2005

A BOOK OF GRACE-FILLED DAYS

LOYOLAPRESS.

CHICAGO

LOYOLAPRESS.

3441 N. ASHLAND AVENUE
CHICAGO, ILLINOIS 60657
(800) 621-1008
WWW.LOYOLABOOKS.ORG

Cover and interior design by Kathy Kikkert

Library of Congress Cataloging-in-Publication Data
Wright, Vinita Hampton, 1958–
    2005 : a book of grace-filled days / Vinita Hampton Wright.
        p. cm.
    ISBN 0-8294-1973-X
1. Devotional calendars. I. Title: Two thousand five. II. Title.
BV4811.W685 2005
242'.3—dc22

                                        2004001511

Printed in The United States of America

04 05 06 07 08 Bang 10 9 8 7 6 5 4 3 2 1

INTRODUCTION

I was in my twenties and living half a world away from my family, on a yearlong teaching assignment in the Middle East. I had no money to speak of or job to return to, and I was in the midst of a difficult transition, because problems with my voice required that I shift from a music career to something else. And recently I'd been dealt a blow in the romance department.

At that time I had not yet been introduced to the lectionary, but it was my habit to read a psalm every day; in this way I read through the book of Psalms every few months. One morning I was reading Psalm 42, and my gaze lingered on the verse "Yet the Lord will command his lovingkindness in the day time, and in the night his song shall be with me . . ." (King James Version). I could not leave that verse. The idea of a song in the night intrigued me. And relieved me. Even in this dark time, God was putting songs in my soul. In fact, my specific struggles were probably composing unique songs of grace. With that realization I began to heal and move ahead in my life with more hope.

Scripture was given to us for many reasons, and one of its purposes is our daily nourishment. The Bible helps us because its wisdom is timeless. It encourages us because its stories and lessons mirror the situations we face today. It sharpens us because it is truthful about the human condition. It teaches us through its characters, who are exactly like us. And it increases our faith by setting before us glorious visions of the people God created us to be.

One of the great wonders of holy Scripture is that it is many-leveled; we never understand all of its meanings at any one reading. I might read Psalm 42 today and be helped in a different way than I was twenty years ago. No matter how many times we read a particular passage, there will always be more to gain from reading it again. The church understood this early on and designed the lectionary, which leads us through the reading of Scripture repeatedly, season after season and year after year.

One advantage of the lectionary is that when we follow it we aren't as likely to manipulate our reading according to how we feel on a particular day or what book of the Bible we're most interested in. We read through the psalms and the Gospels consistently. We are compelled to consider passages that are not easy or comfortable to consider. We get acquainted with a variety of biblical characters and situations rather than dwell on the few we already know.

And each day we are reading what Christians all over the world are reading. There's something encouraging about that—it's a grand way to participate in the communion of saints.

The Scripture quotations in this book are short; the meditations are, too. Each day's readings will take only a few moments. But I have attempted to take a single aspect from each day's Scripture and illuminate or emphasize it briefly in the meditation. So every day there is a glimpse of God's love and truth as they apply to ordinary life.

May this grace-filled year unfold for you, day by day, in wisdom and peace. May God's word open within you many songs and stories of your own.

[I]t is the hour now for you to awake from sleep. For our salvation is nearer now than when we first believed; the night is advanced, the day is at hand.

—ROMANS 13:11–12

To be eager for the future, hardly able to sleep for anticipation; to look forward with joy and be sure that day is coming—this is the posture our souls were created for. Our grand calling is to be creatures of hope.

Isaiah 2:1–5
Psalm 122
Romans 13:11–14
Matthew 24:37–44

For over all, his glory will be shelter and protection:
shade from the parching heat of day,
refuge and cover from storm and rain.

—ISAIAH 4:6

I understood the meaning of "heat wave" for the first time several summers ago, when hundreds of my fellow Chicagoans died from exposure to unrelenting high temperatures. I am more conscious now of how I am constantly sheltered from the elements. Undoubtedly God's grace shelters my spirit all the time, and I barely perceive it.

Isaiah 4:2–6
Psalm 122
Matthew 8:5–11

Tuesday

NOVEMBER 30

• SAINT ANDREW, APOSTLE •

As he was walking by the Sea of Galilee, he saw two brothers, Simon who is called Peter, and his brother Andrew, casting a net into the sea; they were fishermen. He said to them, "Come after me, and I will make you fishers of men." At once they left their nets and followed him.

—MATTHEW 4:18–20

What prepared Simon and Andrew for this encounter? How did their personal histories lead to their saying yes right then and there? And where is my own history leading me? What encounter is about to change my life?

Romans 10:9–18
Psalm 19
Matthew 4:18–22

Wednesday

DECEMBER 1

Then he took the seven loaves and the fish, gave thanks, broke the loaves, and gave them to the disciples, who in turn gave them to the crowds. They all ate and were satisfied. They picked up the fragments left over— seven baskets full.

—MATTHEW 15:36–37

Within our lives there are probably many fragments of God's blessings—fragments we have yet to recognize or gather. When God blesses, there is abundance—and glorious leftovers!

Isaiah 25:6–10
Psalm 23
Matthew 15:29–37

⇒ 4 ⇐

DECEMBER 2

He humbles those in high places,
and the lofty city he brings down;
He tumbles it to the ground,
levels it with the dust.
—ISAIAH 26:5

Holy God, help the people of my city learn to know you.
May we practice wisdom and mercy and thus avoid harsh
correction.

Isaiah 26:1–6
Psalm 118
Matthew 7:21, 24–27

"Come," says my heart, "seek God's face";
your face, LORD, do I seek!
—PSALM 27:8

Many times I've watched a child look eagerly for a parent's face—around a doorway or a blanket held up in play. No other body part suffices; the child isn't satisfied until Mom's eyes or Dad's mouth comes into view. Well, my heart understands that it's not enough to see God's works and wisdom. The heart longs for communion that is achieved only by looking into the eyes of another. For intimacy of spirit, I need to see the face of God—the unmistakable character of love and holiness.

Isaiah 29:17–24
Psalm 27
Matthew 9:27–31

DECEMBER 4

No longer will your Teacher hide himself,
but with your own eyes you shall see your Teacher,
While from behind, a voice shall sound in your ears:
"This is the way; walk in it,"
when you would turn to the right or to the left.

—ISAIAH 30:20–21

Where would we be without the guidance of others? What dangerous detours might we take? We have voices all around us, of friends and family, pastors and teachers—not only of people in our lives today but also of those who came before us. All we have to do is listen.

Isaiah 30:19–21, 23–26
Psalm 147
Matthew 9:35–10:1, 5–8

DECEMBER 5

• SECOND SUNDAY OF ADVENT •

The spirit of the LORD shall rest upon him:
a spirit of wisdom and of understanding,
A spirit of counsel and of strength,
a spirit of knowledge and of fear of the LORD.

—ISAIAH 11:2

Dear Jesus, may this spirit rest on me, too. I want to be wise, to understand the world, to do the right thing, and to be strong in all the right ways. You have brought this spirit to me—all I have to do is welcome it into my life every day.

Isaiah 11:1–10
Psalm 72
Romans 15:4–9
Matthew 3:1–12

I will listen for the word of God;
surely the LORD will proclaim peace
To his people, to the faithful,
to those who trust in him.

—PSALM 85:9

Lord, if we can't count on you to help us, who else can we turn to? We trust you; we expect good gifts from you. And the one voice we strain to hear is yours.

Isaiah 35:1–10
Psalm 85
Luke 5:17–26

DECEMBER 7

• SAINT AMBROSE, BISHOP AND DOCTOR OF THE CHURCH •

A voice cries out:
In the desert prepare the way of the LORD!
Make straight in the wasteland a highway for our God!
—ISAIAH 40:3

The road that wound up the hill to our mission hospital was badly eroded, at times nearly impassable. Then the king of that small Middle Eastern country made plans to visit the hospital. And voilà!—the government repaired and paved the road in record time. When the company is important enough, we prepare the way. We do the repair work that we've put off for years. What cleanup would we undertake in our lives if we truly believed that *God is coming?*

Isaiah 40:1–11
Psalm 96
Matthew 18:12–14

Wednesday
DECEMBER 8

• THE IMMACULATE CONCEPTION OF THE BLESSED VIRGIN MARY •

And the angel said to her in reply, "The holy Spirit will come upon you, and the power of the Most High will overshadow you. Therefore the child to be born will be called holy, the Son of God."

—LUKE 1:35

Mary said yes to being "overshadowed" by the Most High. Although we don't expect this to happen to another human being, it is important to ask ourselves, "If the Holy Spirit truly overwhelmed me, what would I give up, and what might I create?"

Genesis 3:9–15, 20
Psalm 98
Ephesians 1:3–6, 11–12
Luke 1:26–38

Amen, I say to you, among those born of women there has been none greater than John the Baptist; yet the least in the kingdom of heaven is greater than he.

—MATTHEW 11:11

Juan Diego was a poor, humble man whose faithfulness brought him to sainthood. Is it possible that I, too, am a saint in the making? What power and wisdom do I have that I don't yet recognize? Am I already a heavenly creature who continues to live as if I am human and nothing more?

Isaiah 41:13–20
Psalm 145
Matthew 11:11–15

*To what shall I compare this generation? It is like children who sit in
marketplaces and call to one another, "We played the flute for you, but
you did not dance, we sang a dirge but you did not mourn."*

—MATTHEW 11:16–17

Lord, when you challenge me to be holy, I feel pressured
and put-upon. When you say, "Be glad—because I love
you!" I'm sure there's some catch and you can't possibly
mean it. It seems I'm always insisting on my own way, my
own interpretation of events. It's easier to doubt and resist
you than to trust you. Help me let go of everything and
simply believe what you say.

Isaiah 48:17–19
Psalm 1
Matthew 11:16–19

DECEMBER 11

*You are destined, it is written, in time to come
to put an end to wrath before the day of the LORD,
To turn back the hearts of fathers toward their sons,
and to re-establish the tribes of Jacob.*

—SIRACH 48:10

So often it seems that the key to harmony within a nation is found in the family. If families hold together, the society will also. How important it is to nurture families in whatever way we can—through parish ministries, public programs, and personal encouragement.

Sirach 48:1–4, 9–11
Psalm 80
Matthew 17:9–13

DECEMBER 12

You too must be patient. Make your hearts firm, because the coming of the Lord is at hand. . . . Take as an example of hardship and patience, brothers, the prophets who spoke in the name of the Lord.

—JAMES 5:8, 10

Long before the civil rights movement in the United States, individual Americans were appealing to the masses to treat all people as equals. What truth do we need to speak about today even though few people will be receptive to it?

Isaiah 35:1–6, 10
Psalm 146
James 5:7–10
Matthew 11:2–11

The utterance of Balaam, son of Beor,
the utterance of the man whose eye is true,
The utterance of one who hears what God says,
and knows what the Most High knows,
Of one who sees what the Almighty sees,
enraptured, and with eyes unveiled.

—NUMBERS 24:3–4

People were naturally drawn to Linda because she seemed to have such a strong connection to God. They trusted her to be truthful and kind. They sensed her wisdom and felt completely safe with her. At the same time, they weren't always eager to hear what she had to say. Linda's presence required people to pay attention to their lives. Such is the way of a prophet.

Numbers 24:2–7, 15–17
Psalm 25
Matthew 21:23–27

DECEMBER 14

Woe to the city, rebellious and polluted,
to the tyrannical city!
She hears no voice,
accepts no correction;
In the LORD she has not trusted,
to her God she has not drawn near.

—ZEPHANIAH 3:1–2

Those verses in Zephaniah describe my town, my country, my whole world. Lord, show me how to live in a different way. I want to follow you, to listen to and take instruction from you, to trust and draw near to you.

Zephaniah 3:1–2, 9–13
Psalm 34
Matthew 21:28–32

Wednesday

DECEMBER 15

For thus says the LORD,
The creator of the heavens,
who is God,
The designer and maker of the earth
who established it,
Not creating it to be a waste,
but designing it to be lived in:
I am the LORD, and there is no other.

—ISAIAH 45:18

God created a home for us. God made a place for people to dwell and taste God's goodness and sense God's love. Help us, Lord, to look more carefully at the ground and the sky, to be more mindful when we breathe fresh air. Help us dwell wholeheartedly in this good life.

Isaiah 45:6–8, 18, 21–25
Psalm 85
Luke 7:18–23

DECEMBER 16

Raise a glad cry, you barren one who did not bear,
break forth in jubilant song, you who were not in labor,
For more numerous are the children of the deserted wife
than the children of her who has a husband,
says the LORD.

—ISAIAH 54:1

Women who cannot have children know that nothing can compensate for their childlessness. But Isaiah seems to speak of a much larger reality, a world in which barren women are mothers to many. Our gift of nurture will not be wasted. In God's eyes, the childless woman is just as honored as the woman with a houseful of children. The grace of God is larger than our neediness, our emptiness, even our most overwhelming grief.

Isaiah 54:1–10
Psalm 30
Luke 7:24–30

O God, give your judgment to the king;
your justice to the son of kings;
That he may govern your people with justice,
your oppressed with right judgment.

—PSALM 72:1–2

Today is a good day to pray this psalm for leaders in both
our church and our government.

Genesis 49:2, 8–10
Psalm 72
Matthew 1:1–17

DECEMBER 18

*Now this is how the birth of Jesus Christ came about. When his mother
Mary was betrothed to Joseph, but before they lived together, she was
found with child through the holy Spirit.*

—MATTHEW 1:18

You see, God sometimes breaks all the rules. A virgin
became pregnant by the Holy Spirit. An angel convinced
her husband-to-be that it was all right, that he should
marry her anyway. So this good Jewish man went along
with a scheme that disregarded physical realities and
religious regulations. What an adventurous beginning to
the life of our Lord! Should anything surprise us after that?

Jeremiah 23:5–8
Psalm 72
Matthew 1:18–25

Again the LORD spoke to Ahaz: Ask for a sign from the LORD, your God; let it be deep as the nether world, or high as the sky! . . . Therefore the Lord himself will give you this sign: the virgin shall be with child, and bear a son, and shall name him Immanuel.

—ISAIAH 7:10–11, 14

Ahaz couldn't accept that it was appropriate to ask for a sign from God, even though God invited him to do so. I imagine God saying, in our day, "Think bigger! Ask for the impossible! I enjoy giving you more than you can dream of—why are you so shy?" But asking for the impossible isn't the only hurdle. Once we ask, we must be prepared for how it might change us.

Isaiah 7:10–14
Psalm 24
Romans 1:1–7
Matthew 1:18–24

DECEMBER 20

"And behold, Elizabeth, your relative, has also conceived a son in her old age, and this is the sixth month for her who was called barren; for nothing will be impossible for God." Mary said, "Behold, I am the handmaid of the Lord. May it be done to me according to your word." Then the angel departed from her.

—LUKE 1:36–38

When I was younger, I didn't see how important it was for Mary to have female company at this critical time. Now I better understand how women help one another. God performed reproductive miracles in another woman— someone Mary knew and trusted—so that she would not be alone. As an added benefit, the older Elizabeth brought a life of wisdom to this bizarre situation. God has understood sisterhood all along!

Isaiah 7:10–14
Psalm 24
Luke 1:26–38

The LORD, your God, is in your midst,
a mighty savior;
He will rejoice over you with gladness,
and renew you in his love,
He will sing joyfully because of you,
as one sings at festivals.

—ZEPHANIAH 3:17–18

A woman smiling as she celebrates her ninetieth birthday with friends and extended family. General Tommy Franks embracing an American soldier in Iraq. A family laughing tearfully over the birth of a new baby. These are expressions of true joy, but they are mere shadows of God's joy over us when we learn to dwell in his love and grace.

Song of Songs 2:8–14 or Zephaniah 3:14–18
Psalm 33
Luke 1:39–45

DECEMBER 22

He has thrown down the rulers from their thrones
but lifted up the lowly.
The hungry he has filled with good things;
the rich he has sent away empty.

—LUKE 1:52–53

Mary spoke these words when she visited her cousin Elizabeth, rejoicing over not only their miraculous pregnancies but also the overarching plan of God that included them and their unborn sons. How would our lives change if we saw personal events in light of God's love for the world? Do we dare see ourselves as part of a grand scheme to bring justice and love to others?

1 Samuel 1:24–28
1 Samuel 2:1, 4–8
Luke 1:46–56

DECEMBER 23

Lo, I am sending my messenger
to prepare the way before me;
And suddenly there will come to the temple
the LORD whom you seek,
And the messenger of the covenant whom you desire.

—MALACHI 3:1

Have you ever been surprised when you got what you'd been looking for? Do answered prayers shock you? Are you really ready to be given what you desire? God clearly stated through the prophet Malachi that the One people were looking for would suddenly come to the temple. Yet when it happened, they weren't ready for it. Are you?

Malachi 3:1–4, 23–24
Psalm 25
Luke 1:57–66

. . . because of the tender mercy of our God
by which the daybreak from on high will visit us
to shine on those who sit in darkness and death's shadow,
to guide our feet into the path of peace.
—LUKE 1:78–79

Imagine sitting in a cell on death row for years and years.
It's dark and you are completely alone. One day a shaft of
light comes in, bringing warmth with it. And Someone is
standing there to take your hand and lead you gently into
the daylight. You lean against this Person and relearn how
to walk outdoors. You feel a soft breeze, and for the first
time in your life you are at peace.

2 Samuel 7:1–5, 8–12, 14, 16
Psalm 89
Luke 1:67–79

*The people who walked in darkness
have seen a great light;
Upon those who dwelt in the land of gloom
a light has shone. . . .
For a child is born to us, a son is given us;
upon his shoulder dominion rests.
They name him Wonder-Counselor, God-Hero,
Father-Forever, Prince of Peace.*
—ISAIAH 9:1, 5

I who have walked in darkness have been graced with
true light. The Christ child has come to *me* because I
needed a Counselor, a Father-Forever, a Prince of Peace.
The Child was born because I needed the light he could
bring to the world. Yes, this Child belongs to me. He
entered human existence to make my existence bright with
hope and purpose.

Vigil:
Isaiah 62:1–5
Psalm 89
Acts 13:16–17, 22–25
Matthew 1:1–25 or 1:18–25

Midnight:
Isaiah 9:1–6
Psalm 96
Titus 2:11–14
Luke 2:1–14

Dawn:
Isaiah 62:11–12
Psalm 97
Titus 3:4–7
Luke 2:15–20

Day:
Isaiah 52:7–10
Psalm 98
Hebrews 1:1–6
John 1:1–18 or 1:1–5, 9–14

DECEMBER 26

[T]he angel of the Lord appeared to Joseph in a dream and said, "Rise, take the child and his mother, flee to Egypt, and stay there until I tell you. Herod is going to search for the child to destroy him." Joseph rose and took the child and his mother by night and departed for Egypt.

—MATTHEW 2:13–14

The holy family's early days together were shaped by a death threat. (Imagine trying to leave the United States while the FBI is out to kill your child!) Joseph and Mary had to make plans quickly, trust each other completely, and care for a child while running for their lives. The next time your family encounters hard times, remember that desperate journey to Egypt—and trust God to shape your lives even in danger.

Sirach 3:2–7, 12–14
Psalm 128
Colossians 3:12–21 or 3:12–17
Matthew 2:13–15, 19–23

DECEMBER 27

• SAINT JOHN, APOSTLE AND EVANGELIST •

[T]he life was made visible;
we have seen it and testify to it
and proclaim to you the eternal life
that was with the Father and was made visible to us.

—1 JOHN 1:2

I made my first apple pie years ago while living in a foreign country. I made it from memory—of the many pies I had watched my mother make. It turned out just fine. Sometimes all we have to guide us is the memory of how someone else lived. St. John's memories of Jesus helped shape the early church, and they continue to guide us, many generations later.

1 John 1:1–4
Psalm 97
John 20:1–8

DECEMBER 28

When Herod realized that he had been deceived by the magi, he became furious. He ordered the massacre of all the boys in Bethlehem and its vicinity two years old and under, in accordance with the time he had ascertained from the magi.

—MATTHEW 2:16

Possibly the cruelest pain on earth is that of a mother having to watch her child die. Yet, again and again, children are massacred by rebel armies, by fanatics, by enemies in different ethnic groups. How might the world change if every time we made a decision, we reflected on how it would affect the children of this generation and the next?

1 John 1:5–2:2
Psalm 124
Matthew 2:13–18

Wednesday

DECEMBER 29

• SAINT THOMAS BECKET, BISHOP AND MARTYR •

Whoever says he is in the light, yet hates his brother, is still in the darkness.

—1 JOHN 2:9

This line from John's letter presents one of the Bible's most difficult truths to accept. Darkness and light cannot coexist. And one form of darkness is hatred toward another person. This is why it is hard to grow spiritually when we harbor grudges or concentrate on the negative qualities in others. Lord, help us give up hate so that we can live in your light.

1 John 2:3–11
Psalm 96
Luke 2:22–35

When they had fulfilled all the prescriptions of the law of the Lord, they returned to Galilee, to their own town of Nazareth. The child grew and became strong, filled with wisdom; and the favor of God was upon him.

—LUKE 2:39–40

It's important to note that Jesus' life developed right in his hometown. The holy family simply returned to their normal environment, and that's where our Savior grew up. We usually don't fulfill our life calling by seeking some exotic location or special set of circumstances. We are formed right where we are, in the midst of ordinary life.

1 John 2:12–17
Psalm 96
Luke 2:36–40

Friday

DECEMBER 31

• SAINT SYLVESTER I, POPE • NEW YEAR'S EVE •

But to those who did accept him he gave power to become children of God, to those who believe in his name, who were born not by natural generation nor by human choice nor by a man's decision but of God.

—JOHN 1:12–13

We have the privilege of being God's children, and we can't claim any credit for it. God chose us. What choice is ours? To accept the love and grace offered us. All we can do is say yes to the God who loves us. When we do, our lives are transformed.

1 John 2:18–21
Psalm 96
John 1:1–18

⋛ 35 ⋚

JANUARY 1

As proof that you are children, God sent the spirit of his Son into our hearts, crying out, "Abba, Father!"
—GALATIANS 4:6

There is a reason we experience so many emotions toward God. Long ago, a spirit was sent into our hearts that recognizes God as parent. The next time you feel anticipation, anger, longing, hurt, anxiety, or playfulness in your relationship with God, consider it part of your natural response as son or daughter.

Numbers 6:22–27
Psalm 67
Galatians 4:4–7
Luke 2:16–21

Sunday

JANUARY 2

• THE EPIPHANY OF THE LORD •

When Jesus was born in Bethlehem of Judea, in the days of King Herod, behold, magi from the east arrived in Jerusalem, saying, "Where is the newborn king of the Jews? We saw his star at its rising and have come to do him homage."

—MATTHEW 2:1–2

People from far away understood who Jesus was, but many people close by did not even know that a King had arrived. Do we recognize God's blessings only at a distance? Must we travel far in order to find grace or meaning or purpose? How attentive are we to the treasures that are right beside us—or even within us?

Isaiah 60:1–6
Psalm 72
Ephesians 3:2–3, 5–6
Matthew 2:1–12

[T]he people who sit in darkness
have seen a great light,
on those dwelling in a land overshadowed by death
light has arisen.
—MATTHEW 4:16

On the day Amy began to believe that God loved her, the world took on a new brightness. Colors were richer; people were more interesting; the air itself seemed kind. In discovering love, she threw off the fears and burdens that had made existence dark and hard to bear. She described it to a friend: "It's like stepping out of a dark room into daytime—for the first time."

1 John 3:22–4:6
Psalm 2
Matthew 4:12–17, 23–25

———————

JANUARY 4

• SAINT ELIZABETH ANN SETON, RELIGIOUS •

When [Jesus] disembarked and saw the vast crowd, his heart was moved with pity for them, for they were like sheep without a shepherd; and he began to teach them many things.

—MARK 6:34

Widowed before she was thirty, Elizabeth Ann Seton and her five children were forced into a life of poverty. She converted to Catholicism in the early nineteenth century and not long afterward initiated the parochial school system in America by establishing the first Catholic girls' school. She then founded a religious order, the Sisters of Charity, to help with the school. Despite her own struggles and sorrows, Elizabeth Ann Seton was able to look out at the "vast crowd" of children and see their needs. Her compassion enabled her to accomplish amazing works.

1 John 4:7–10
Psalm 72
Mark 6:34–44

There is no fear in love, but perfect love drives out fear because fear has to do with punishment, and so one who fears is not yet perfect in love.

—1 JOHN 4:18

Early in their history, the Jesuits recognized that the best leaders were those who loved the people under their direction. These leaders did not motivate people through fear of punishment or failure. They believed that demonstrating confidence in another person's ability would enable that person to grow and to accomplish God's work in the world.

1 John 4:11–18
Psalm 72
Mark 6:45–52

If anyone says, "I love God," but hates his brother, he is a liar; for whoever does not love a brother whom he has seen cannot love God whom he has not seen.

—1 JOHN 4:20

In the film *Jesus of Nazareth,* a scene occurs between Simon Peter, a "blue-collar" fisherman, and Matthew, a tax collector for the occupying government. Simon and Matthew are fellow Jews who both want to be followers of Jesus. Peter despises Matthew in the way that so many working-class people despise "the tax man." Although the scene is a fictionalized account, it shows us how love must have been tested among even those who were closest to Jesus.

1 John 4:19–5:4
Psalm 72
Luke 4:14–22

Friday

JANUARY 7

• SAINT RAYMOND OF PEÑAFORT, PRIEST •

The report about him spread all the more, and great crowds assembled to listen to him and to be cured of their ailments, but he would withdraw to deserted places to pray.

—LUKE 5:15–16

Sophie's ministry to battered women had quickly expanded; in addition to directing two safe houses, she was traveling regularly to speaking engagements. One afternoon an old friend who'd been a social worker for years stopped her cold. "If you don't nurture your own spiritual life, you'll soon run out of resources for all the women you're helping." Grateful for the candid advice, Sophie reworked her schedule to include "soul time."

1 John 5:5–13
Psalm 147
Luke 5:12–16

We know that we belong to God, and the whole world is under the power of the evil one. We also know that the Son of God has come and has given us discernment to know the one who is true.

—1 JOHN 5:19–20

He had always talked disparagingly of lawyers—until a false charge was brought against him. Standing before a judge in the confusing courtroom environment, he was immensely grateful for the attorney beside him who not only understood the legal language flying around them but also knew how the system worked. It is no small thing to have an advocate when you must get along in a hostile world.

1 John 5:14–21
Psalm 149
John 3:22–30

Sunday

JANUARY 9

• THE BAPTISM OF THE LORD •

A bruised reed he shall not break,
and a smoldering wick he shall not quench.

—ISAIAH 42:3

The next time you feel bruised and as if you're about to give up, remember that God wants to heal you. The next time you are nearly out of energy and ideas, remember that God is ready to fan your smoldering life back into flame. Even when you assume you're of little use, God does not consider giving up on you.

Isaiah 42:1–4, 6–7
Psalm 29
Acts 10:34–38
Matthew 3:13–17

*In times past, God spoke in partial and various ways to our ancestors
through the prophets; in these last days, he spoke to us through a son,
whom he made heir of all things and through whom he created the
universe.*

—HEBREWS 1:1–2

How radical it was for God to send Jesus to speak to us
directly and to live as a flesh-and-blood example for us.
When theology and theory become confusing, it is always
safe to turn to Jesus.

Hebrews 1:1–6
Psalm 97
Mark 1:14–20

JANUARY 11

The people were astonished at [Jesus'] teaching, for he taught them as one having authority and not as the scribes.

—MARK 1:22

Take a moment to remember the teachers you most admired and respected. They probably earned your respect not because they were heavy-handed but because they lived what they taught. Consider those who observe your life—your own children, your colleagues, or even people in your community. Do you try to make them look up to you, or does your very life elicit their respect?

Hebrews 2:5–12
Psalm 8
Mark 1:21–28

JANUARY 12

Rising very early before dawn, he left and went off to a deserted place, where he prayed.

—MARK 1:35

By this time in Jesus' life, he knew who he was and the work that was before him. Yet he found it necessary to spend private time with God the Father. If Jesus needed this communion, how much more do we?

Hebrews 2:14–18
Psalm 105
Mark 1:29–39

Encourage yourselves daily while it is still "today," so that none of you may grow hardened by the deceit of sin.

—HEBREWS 3:13

What does it mean to grow hardened by the deceit of sin? Is that what happens when my conscience isn't so sensitive anymore? When lying or gossiping no longer makes me feel guilty? How can I encourage my own soul so that I don't slip into the habit of rationalizing questionable thoughts and actions? Daily prayer can help. In order not to become spiritually hardened, I need to grow tenderhearted toward God.

Hebrews 3:7–14
Psalm 95
Mark 1:40–45

JANUARY 14

They were not to be like their ancestors,
a rebellious and defiant generation,
A generation whose heart was not constant,
whose spirit was not faithful to God.

—PSALM 78:8

Is it possible to change the course of history? Can we take a family, a community, or even a nation in a new direction simply by correcting in ourselves what was so damaging in the generations that came before us? Perhaps our prayers and efforts are too limited. We can dare to ask God to help us bring entire groups of souls to a better way of life.

Hebrews 4:1–5, 11
Psalm 78
Mark 2:1–12

Jesus . . . said to them [that], "Those who are well do not need a physician, but the sick do. I did not come to call the righteous but sinners."

—MARK 2:17

There's an old joke about a man who tries to join the local church but is rejected repeatedly for one reason or another. Finally he prays, "Lord, I don't know how to please these people. What can I do?" The Lord replies, "I don't know. I've been trying to get into that church for years myself." When we reject people because they don't "measure up," we take ourselves out of God's company.

Hebrews 4:12–16
Psalm 19
Mark 2:13–17

JANUARY 16

I did not know him, but the one who sent me to baptize with water told me, "On whomever you see the Spirit come down and remain, he is the one who will baptize with the holy Spirit."

—JOHN 1:33

Lord, help us recognize your servants when they come to us. Open our eyes to see your holiness in others, and move our hearts to support them as they do your work.

Isaiah 49:3, 5–6
Psalm 40
1 Corinthians 1:1–3
John 1:29–34

JANUARY 17

Yours is princely power from the day of your birth.

—PSALM 110:3

This psalm may refer to King David or to the Messiah to come. But as a Christian, a person spiritually reborn, you, too, are a child of God. When is your spiritual birthday? You may consider it the day of your baptism or your confirmation. What difference does it make to you that you are part of this royal family called the church? How might that identity affect the way you go through a typical day?

Hebrews 5:1–10
Psalm 110
Mark 2:18–22

JANUARY 18

The fear of the LORD is the beginning of wisdom;
prudent are all who live by it.

—PSALM 111:10

As a child, I had a healthy fear of my father. I was
accountable to him for my behavior. He expected me to be
honest, sensible, and moral. Those expectations indeed
shaped the way I lived my life, well into adulthood. In the
same way, our lives should be shaped by the expectations
of our heavenly Father, to whom we will ultimately answer.
This sort of "fear," rather than scaring and oppressing us,
actually guides and protects us.

Hebrews 6:10–20
Psalm 111
Mark 2:23–28

JANUARY 19

[Jesus] said to them, "Is it lawful to do good on the sabbath rather than to do evil, to save life rather than to destroy it?" But they remained silent. Looking around at them with anger and grieved at their hardness of heart, he said to the man, "Stretch out your hand." He stretched it out and his hand was restored.

—MARK 3:4–5

Bob's mother seemed to want him to stay ill—when he was sick he was at home with her and she could keep an eye on him. He knew she loved him, but it was an unhealthy love born of her own neediness. The day he realized this, he decided to move out. He needed to be with people whose love might be tougher but would urge him to better health and a fuller life.

Hebrews 7:1–3, 15–17
Psalm 110
Mark 3:1–6

He has no need, as did the high priests, to offer sacrifice day after day, first for his own sins and then for those of the people; he did that once for all when he offered himself.

—HEBREWS 7:27

Do you ever have that vague sense that you owe somebody something—money, an apology, a better performance, a returned phone call? A sense of justice is born into most of us; in the back of our minds is a tally of what we owe others and what they owe us. But, ultimately, we cannot make things even. We can rely only on the life, death, and resurrection of Christ. His passion was the final reckoning.

Hebrews 7:25–8:6
Psalm 40
Mark 3:7–12

I will put my laws in their minds
and I will write them upon their hearts.
I will be their God,
and they shall be my people.

—HEBREWS 8:10

For generations, the Israelites had been admonished
frequently to memorize and obey God's laws. God's
prophet Jeremiah (quoted here in Hebrews) had a vision.
He saw a future in which God's ways were part of our
character rather than lessons we must learn. We can be
confident of this vision. We can be so confident that we
call ourselves, even now, God's people.

Hebrews 8:6–13
Psalm 85
Mark 3:13–19

[Jesus] came home. Again [the] crowd gathered, making it impossible for them even to eat. When his relatives heard of this they set out to seize him, for they said, "He is out of his mind."

—MARK 3:20–21

How important to you is "balance"? Have you ever followed a conviction to the point that people thought you were taking things too far? Have your responsibilities ever required that you lose sleep, upset the status quo, or ignore people who thought you should be spending time with them? If so, you are in good company. Jesus shows us that sometimes the faith-filled life will not appear normal to society.

Hebrews 9:2–3, 11–14
Psalm 47
Mark 3:20–21

JANUARY 23

I urge you, brothers, in the name of our Lord Jesus Christ, that all of you agree in what you say, and that there be no divisions among you, but that you be united in the same mind and in the same purpose.

—1 CORINTHIANS 1:10

From the very beginning, unity has been difficult to maintain in Christ's church. Yet divisions among Christians prevent us from being effective in God's work. Think of one issue in the church that you feel strongly about. Make a point to have coffee with someone in the church who does not share your opinion. Look for ways to love that person and thus further Christ's love in your community.

Isaiah 8:23–9:3
Psalm 27
1 Corinthians 1:10–13, 17
Matthew 4:12–23 or 4:12–17

Just as it is appointed that human beings die once, and after this the judgment, so also Christ, offered once to take away the sins of many, will appear a second time, not to take away sin but to bring salvation to those who eagerly await him.

—HEBREWS 9:27–28

Lord, I keep thinking that when I meet you I will have to account for my sins, but you have already taken them away. Our meeting will be one of joy. Help me live in anticipation, rather than in fear, of that moment.

Hebrews 9:15, 24–28
Psalm 98
Mark 3:22–30

JANUARY 25

• THE CONVERSION OF SAINT PAUL, APOSTLE •

*[Saul] stayed some days with the disciples in Damascus, and he began
at once to proclaim Jesus in the synagogues, that he is the Son of God.
All who heard him were astounded and said, "Is not this the man who
in Jerusalem ravaged those who call upon this name, and came here
expressly to take them back in chains to the chief priests?"*

—ACTS 9:19–21

Decades ago, a young Communist living in Syria entered a
church in order to cause trouble and disperse the
worshipers. Instead, the young man's heart was changed,
and that night he became a follower of Jesus. When I met
him he had been the pastor of a church in another country
for many years. It seems that the more antagonistic we are,
the more astounded we are when we encounter God's love.

Acts 22:3–16 or 9:1–22
Psalm 117
Mark 16:15–18

I remind you to stir into flame the gift of God that you have. . . . For God did not give us a spirit of cowardice but rather of power and love and self-control.

—2 TIMOTHY 1:6–7

In my work with writers, I see over and over again how our gifts become sources of power, wisdom, and love. When we develop our gifts, we experience joy and extend that joy to others. What are your gifts? Do you dare stir them up, as you would stir smoldering ashes into flame? Will you allow fear to hold you back from doing what you are gifted to do?

2 Timothy 1:1–8 or Titus 1:1–5
Psalm 110
Mark 4:1–20

JANUARY 27

Let us hold unwaveringly to our confession that gives us hope, for he who made the promise is trustworthy.

—HEBREWS 10:23

When they crossed the border, the refugees had only a name, an address, and the assurance "You can trust this family. They will hide you and give you whatever you need." Thus have many refugees through the ages found safety. Without trustworthy people, hope would be lost. This is the way we cling to God's word—as wayfarers who must rely on the One who can be trusted.

Hebrews 10:19–25
Psalm 24
Mark 4:21–25

You need endurance to do the will of God and receive what he has promised. . . . We are not among those who draw back and perish, but among those who have faith and will possess life.

—HEBREWS 10:36, 39

What helps you endure? What vision keeps you going on the tough days? The varied situations in life will sometimes require more patience and strength than you have. But these qualities will grow in you through faith in God's goodness. Find God's promises—in the Bible and in the stories of God's people—and allow those visions to sustain you.

Hebrews 10:32–39
Psalm 37
Mark 4:26–34

JANUARY 29

By faith Abraham obeyed when he was called to go out to a place that he was to receive as an inheritance; he went out, not knowing where he was to go.

—HEBREWS 11:8

He didn't know where the money would come from, who would help him, or how long it would take—all he had was the conviction that he had important work to do. And each day, each week, each month, he managed to find the money, the help, and the time. It wasn't a simple process, just a steady one—and his vision and faith made it possible.

Hebrews 11:1–2, 8–19
Luke 1:69–75
Mark 4:35–41

JANUARY 30

Blessed are the poor in spirit,
for theirs is the kingdom of heaven.
Blessed are they who mourn,
for they will be comforted.
—MATTHEW 5:3–4

God does good work in our souls when we are poor in spirit and when we mourn. Yet we try to avoid difficult times that humble us or surround us with grief. Our goal is to change the situation, to "get better" fast, but Jesus says that we are actually blessed when life is hard. We won't always be down-and-out. The comfort will come.

Zephaniah 2:3; 3:12–13
Psalm 146
1 Corinthians 1:26–31
Matthew 5:1–12

Monday

JANUARY 31

• SAINT JOHN BOSCO, PRIEST •

As they approached Jesus, they caught sight of the man who had been possessed by Legion, sitting there clothed and in his right mind. And they were seized with fear. . . . Then they began to beg [Jesus] to leave their district.

—MARK 5:15, 17

People often remain in unhealthy situations because it is actually more frightening to them to face a new set of choices and responsibilities. The terrible situation seems easier simply because it is familiar. God wants something better for us—total freedom and a life that is open to grace. Are the adjustments we would need to make in order to enjoy a better life really more frightening than the results of sinful patterns in our lives?

Hebrews 11:32–40
Psalm 31
Mark 5:1–20

FEBRUARY 1

[Jesus] said to her, "Daughter, your faith has saved you. Go in peace and be cured of your affliction."

—MARK 5:34

In several Gospel accounts, Jesus heals a person while also forgiving the person's sins. He understood that the physical and spiritual are intertwined. When we are physically ill, it is a signal to pay attention to our souls as well. And when we suffer from depression, anxiety, or other ills of the mind and heart, our physical lives are probably in need of healing, too.

Hebrews 12:1–4
Psalm 22
Mark 5:21–43

Simeon blessed them and said to Mary his mother, "Behold, this child is destined for the fall and rise of many in Israel, and to be a sign that will be contradicted (and you yourself a sword will pierce) so that the thoughts of many hearts may be revealed."

—LUKE 2:34–35

Mary had the honor of being the mother of Jesus, but that honor would bring suffering with it. Think about your own life calling. What about it is honorable and joyful? What pain and conflict might arise in your life if you follow the path God has for you?

Malachi 3:1–4
Psalm 24
Hebrews 2:14–18
Luke 2:22–40 or 2:22–32

[Y]ou have approached Mount Zion and the city of the living God, the heavenly Jerusalem, and countless angels in festal gathering, and the assembly of the firstborn enrolled in heaven, and God the judge of all, and the spirits of the just made perfect, and Jesus, the mediator of a new covenant.

—HEBREWS 12:22–24

Our faith is filled with mystery and with visions that seem magical to us now. But we can open ourselves to this mystery by exercising our imaginations more often, by reading more fairy tales, by stretching our minds beyond this world. What God has prepared for us we cannot even grasp, but we can certainly dream and thus prepare our spirits for the time to come.

Hebrews 12:18–19, 21–24
Psalm 48
Mark 6:7–13

Let mutual love continue. Do not neglect hospitality, for through it some have unknowingly entertained angels.

—HEBREWS 13:1–2

For three generations the Davis family has set an extra place at their table on Sundays and every holiday. Because family members are aware of this extra place, very often one of them invites a guest. In this way they have entertained college students who were alone on holidays, people who visited their church that day, homeless people, families going through tough times, and—who knows?— probably an angel or two.

Hebrews 13:1–8
Psalm 27
Mark 6:14–29

The apostles gathered together with Jesus and reported all they had done and taught. He said to them, "Come away by yourselves to a deserted place and rest a while." People were coming and going in great numbers, and they had no opportunity even to eat.

—MARK 6:30–31

There comes a time when you have given all you can, and you must rest and regroup. When you are depleted and people are still making demands on you, remember Jesus' care for his disciples and go away by yourself to a deserted place and rest awhile.

Hebrews 13:15–17, 20–21
Psalm 23
Mark 6:30–34

FEBRUARY 6

I came to you in weakness and fear and much trembling, and my message and my proclamation were not with persuasive [words of] wisdom, but with a demonstration of spirit and power, so that your faith might rest not on human wisdom but on the power of God.

—1 CORINTHIANS 2:3–5

Most of us have been in a situation in which someone needed our help or advice and we did not feel qualified to give it. But when we are walking in faith, our inadequacies are not nearly as important as our love. Genuine love is always bolstered by the power of God.

Isaiah 58:7–10
Psalm 112
1 Corinthians 2:1–5
Matthew 5:13–16

FEBRUARY 7

Whatever villages or towns or countryside he entered, they laid the sick
in the marketplaces and begged him that they might touch only the
tassel on his cloak; and as many as touched it were healed.

—MARK 6:56

In the early days of Christianity, and still today, pilgrims
traveled to holy sites in order to be healed, and sometimes
miracles happened. Of course, we don't have to travel to
seek God's mercy—we can pursue it right where we are.
What healing do you need—physical, mental, spiritual,
emotional—and how might you seek God here and now?

Genesis 1:1–19
Psalm 104
Mark 6:53–56

FEBRUARY 8

• SAINT JEROME EMILIANI, PRIEST • SAINT JOSEPHINE BAKHITA, VIRGIN •

You disregard God's commandment but cling to human tradition.
—MARK 7:8

"This is the way we've always done it, and we're not going to change things now." Thus ends many a discussion, whether in the church, at the dinner table, or in Congress. Human tradition allows for evil practices to continue long after people see them for what they are. Some of Jesus' harshest statements were to religious leaders who favored their traditions over God's mercy and justice. We should always ask, "Is this what God really intended?"

Genesis 1:20–2:4
Psalm 8
Mark 7:1–13

Yet even now, says the LORD,
return to me with your whole heart,
with fasting, and weeping, and mourning;
Rend your hearts, not your garments,
and return to the LORD, your God.
For gracious and merciful is he,
slow to anger, rich in kindness,
and relenting in punishment.

—JOEL 2:12–13

As we walk these next few weeks toward Easter, dear Jesus,
help us break open our hearts and offer you our sin, our
grief, our pain, and our hope.

Joel 2:12–18
Psalm 51
2 Corinthians 5:20–6:2
Matthew 6:1–6, 16–18

[W]hoever wishes to save his life will lose it, but whoever loses his life for my sake will save it.

—LUKE 9:24

Many a storybook villain schemes to obtain all the treasure and then dies for his greed. Many a popular movie gives a tragic end to the person who looks out only for herself. Such plots are based on a spiritual reality: when we grasp selfishly at life, we come up empty-handed. Have the courage to say, "God, my life is all yours, and I trust you to take good care of it."

Deuteronomy 30:15–20
Psalm 1
Luke 9:22–25

Friday

FEBRUARY 11

• OUR LADY OF LOURDES •

Cry out full-throated and unsparingly,
lift up your voice like a trumpet blast;
Tell my people their wickedness,
and the house of Jacob their sins.

—ISAIAH 58:1

Sometimes a complacent society can hear only the voices that are loud and disturbing. God sent his prophets to stir up trouble and change the course of history. Who are God's prophets today, and how are we responding to their messages?

Isaiah 58:1–9
Psalm 51
Matthew 9:14–15

Gladden the soul of your servant;
to you, Lord, I lift up my soul.
Lord, you are kind and forgiving,
most loving to all who call on you.

—PSALM 86:4–5

Do I ever turn to God so that my soul can be gladdened?
Or do I usually have some pressing need to present? I turn
to good friends all the time simply because I enjoy their
company. Why not call upon God for the mere pleasure of
spending time with Someone who is kind and forgiving,
Someone who is always loving toward me?

Isaiah 58:9–14
Psalm 86
Luke 5:27–32

Then the devil took him up to a very high mountain, and showed him all the kingdoms of the world in their magnificence, and he said to him, "All these I shall give to you, if you will prostrate yourself and worship me."

—MATTHEW 4:8–9

"If you'll look the other way, we'll owe you one." "If you support our cause, we'll make sure you get elected." "If you lie for me this once, I'll make it up to you, I promise." Temptations come in all forms. How have you been tempted lately?

Genesis 2:7–9; 3:1–7
Psalm 51
Romans 5:12–19 or 5:12, 17–19
Matthew 4:1–11

• SAINT CYRIL, MONK • SAINT METHODIUS, BISHOP • VALENTINE'S DAY •

You shall not go about spreading slander among your kinsmen; nor shall you stand by idly when your neighbor's life is at stake. I am the LORD.
—LEVITICUS 19:16

Americans continue to hear stories of heroic acts that happened on September 11, 2001. We know that if we don't help one another in times of danger, no one will ever be safe. Today as you pass people on the street or in the hallway, cultivate the attitude those Old Testament laws called for by saying in your mind, "You are my neighbor."

Leviticus 19:1–2, 11–18
Psalm 19
Matthew 25:31–46

FEBRUARY 15

If you forgive others their transgressions, your heavenly Father will forgive you. But if you do not forgive others, neither will your Father forgive your transgressions.

—MATTHEW 6:14–15

After seeing a therapist and renewing the habits of Mass attendance and daily prayer, Charlie decided to forgive the former business partner who had cheated him years ago. What surprised Charlie was how much easier it was to forgive once he had decided to do so. And when he gave up the burden of resentment, his spirit felt freer than it had in years. He was able to experience God's forgiveness and love in a way he hadn't been able to for a long time.

Isaiah 55:10–11
Psalm 34
Matthew 6:7–15

While still more people gathered in the crowd, [Jesus] said to them, "This generation is an evil generation; it seeks a sign, but no sign will be given it, except the sign of Jonah. Just as Jonah became a sign to the Ninevites, so will the Son of Man be to this generation."

—LUKE 11:29–30

Why were people "evil" to seek a sign? Because right in front of them was Jesus, whose teachings rang true and whose miracles were evident. This story should lead us to ask ourselves, "What do I already know to be true? And am I living in light of that truth? Or am I looking for excuses to avoid doing the right thing?" The truth can change our lives only when we choose to let it do so.

Jonah 3:1–10
Psalm 51
Luke 11:29–32

Thursday

FEBRUARY 17

Ask and it will be given to you; seek and you will find; knock and the door will be opened to you.

—MATTHEW 7:7

How often do I assume that I won't receive what I want or need or that my request will be denied? Is this the kind of God I have—one who begrudges every gift, one who looks for reasons not to care for me? I think that God would want me to ask for everything rather than shrink back and not anticipate divine generosity.

Esther C:12, 14–16, 23–25
Psalm 138
Matthew 7:7–12

FEBRUARY 18

Do I indeed derive any pleasure from the death of the wicked? says the Lord GOD. Do I not rather rejoice when he turns from his evil way that he may live?

—EZEKIEL 18:23

Ben rooted for the detective in the movie and laughed with satisfaction when the serial killer suffered a brutal death by explosion. It was only later that he realized how the script and special effects had fed his desire for revenge and that grace and mercy had appeared nowhere in the plot. After that, he watched movies more critically.

Ezekiel 18:21–28
Psalm 130
Matthew 5:20–26

Saturday

FEBRUARY 19

Your hands made me and fashioned me;
give me insight to learn your commands.

—PSALM 119:73

If God created us, it follows that we have the innate ability
to learn God's ways. We come from God, and we are going
to God. Our spirits wait to be shaped by God's wisdom
and love.

Deuteronomy 26:16–19
Psalm 119
Matthew 5:43–48

The LORD said to Abram: "Go forth from the land of your kinsfolk and from your father's house to a land that I will show you. . . ."
Abram went as the LORD directed him, and Lot went with him. Abram was seventy-five years old when he left Haran.
—GENESIS 12:1, 4

The first twenty years of Sharon's life were full of abuse and loss. She spent the next twenty years recovering from those early wounds. During her fifth decade she discovered that her stories gave courage to others, so she began speaking to various groups. Well into her "senior" years, she began a career as a spiritual director and teacher. Even when society says we aren't useful anymore, God has good plans for us.

Genesis 12:1–4
Psalm 33
2 Timothy 1:8–10
Matthew 17:1–9

Stop judging and you will not be judged. Stop condemning and you
will not be condemned. Forgive and you will be forgiven.

—LUKE 6:37

Jesus, you made it clear that whatever I do will come back
to me, or, as the saying goes, "What goes around comes
around." The principle is so simple, yet I never quite learn,
do I? Help me measure my words and actions against how I
hope to be treated by others.

Daniel 9:4–10
Psalm 79
Luke 6:36–38

Tend the flock of God in your midst, [overseeing] not by constraint but willingly, as God would have it, not for shameful profit but eagerly. Do not lord it over those assigned to you, but be examples to the flock.

—1 PETER 5:2–3

Fr. Pete has been pastor of the same little church for years. He's a horrible fund-raiser; his sermons aren't particularly astute; and it's well-known that Catherine, the church secretary, oversees much of the parish business. But Fr. Pete is a gentle soul who is so good at leading others that people in his care just naturally become leaders themselves. This is what good shepherds do.

1 Peter 5:1–4
Psalm 23
Matthew 16:13–19

Into your hands I commend my spirit;
you will redeem me, LORD, faithful God.

—PSALM 31:6

Christ said these words from the cross. We would be naive, however, to think that Jesus spoke these words for the first time when he was about to die. He had learned this psalm, memorized it, and rehearsed it throughout his life. We, too, must prepare for death long before we die, by saying often, "Into your hands I commend my spirit."

Jeremiah 18:18–20
Psalm 31
Matthew 20:17–28

Then Abraham said, "If they will not listen to Moses and the prophets, neither will they be persuaded if someone should rise from the dead."
—LUKE 16:31

We sometimes say that we need more proof to believe in God. But, as Jesus points out in this parable, belief is a matter of the heart. When you struggle with doubt, it's fine to explore the rational evidence. But offer your whole self to the mysteries of the universe. Faith can grow in uncertainty, and God's presence will become evident in the heart that is open.

Jeremiah 17:5–10
Psalm 1
Luke 16:19–31

Friday

FEBRUARY 25

Israel loved Joseph best of all his sons, for he was the child of his old age; and he had made him a long tunic. When his brothers saw that their father loved him best of all his sons, they hated him so much that they would not even greet him.

—GENESIS 37:3–4

Most families engage in some version of favoritism, and it always leads to problems. In the Genesis story, Joseph's brothers actually sell him into slavery. We see families every day who are eaten away by sibling rivalry. To preserve family peace, we must take stock of our relationships periodically and heal conflicts whenever we can.

Genesis 37:3–4, 12–13, 17–28
Psalm 105
Matthew 21:33–43, 45–46

The tax collectors and sinners were all drawing near to listen to him,
but the Pharisees and scribes began to complain, saying, "This man
welcomes sinners and eats with them."

—LUKE 15:1–2

The inner-city church had developed effective programs to
help families who lived in the nearby housing projects.
When children from the projects began to attend Sunday
school, however, some church members pulled their kids
out of the class. They worried that the children from the
projects would influence their own children. They were
willing to offer assistance to the poor at a distance; they
just didn't want to be around them.

Micah 7:14–15, 18–20
Psalm 103
Luke 15:1–3, 11–32

Here, then, in their thirst for water, the people grumbled against Moses, saying, "Why did you ever make us leave Egypt? Was it just to have us die here of thirst with our children and our livestock?" So Moses cried out to the LORD, "What shall I do with this people? A little more and they will stone me!"

—EXODUS 17:3–4

This incident happened after God had performed countless miracles in order to free the Hebrews from slavery in Egypt. Then they wandered in the wilderness for forty years, and it seems that they needed that much time to learn how to trust God and stop grumbling. What is *your* wilderness, and what lessons have you learned about trust?

Exodus 17:3–7
Psalm 95
Romans 5:1–2, 5–8
John 4:5–42 or 4:5–15, 19–26, 39–42

The prophet sent him the message: "Go and wash seven times in the Jordan, and your flesh will heal, and you will be clean." But Naaman went away angry, saying, "I thought that he would surely come out and stand there to invoke the LORD his God, and would move his hand over the spot, and thus cure the leprosy."

—2 KINGS 5:10–11

Naaman was like most of us: he wanted God to help him, but he also wanted to dictate exactly *how* God helped him. In the next verses of this passage, Naaman's servants convince him to do as the prophet says, and he is healed. May we be humble enough to accept grace even when it's not on our terms.

2 Kings 5:1–15
Psalm 42
Luke 4:24–30

MARCH 1

Then Peter approaching asked him, "Lord, if my brother sins against me, how often must I forgive him? As many as seven times?" Jesus answered, "I say to you, not seven times but seventy-seven times."
—MATTHEW 18:21–22

Peter was looking for a rule he could follow—and a limit he could live with. But Jesus made it clear that forgiveness is not subject to a formula. We are expected to forgive as many times as it takes to heal the rifts in our relationships.

Daniel 3:25, 34–43
Psalm 25
Matthew 18:21–35

Therefore, I teach you the statutes and decrees as the LORD, my God,
has commanded me. . . . Observe them carefully, for thus will you give
evidence of your wisdom and intelligence to the nations.

—DEUTERONOMY 4:5–6

You can nearly always tell when someone has been raised
to have good manners. In the same way, you can usually
tell, sometimes just by a person's speech, if he or she has
had extensive education. Whatever your training is, it will
speak clearly through your life. This is especially true when
it comes to spiritual formation.

Deuteronomy 4:1, 5–9
Psalm 147
Matthew 5:17–19

Say to them: This is the nation which does not listen to the voice of the LORD, its God, or take correction. Faithfulness has disappeared; the word itself is banished from their speech.

—JEREMIAH 7:28

As God's people, we are called to be faithful to the teachings of Scripture. Such faithfulness requires that we listen to God and submit ourselves to correction. Correction can be painful. But as we experience God's honesty about our faults and sins, we will also experience God's ongoing forgiveness. In this way our faith will grow.

Jeremiah 7:23–28
Psalm 95
Luke 11:14–23

Friday

MARCH 4

• SAINT CASIMIR •

*You shall love the Lord your God with all your heart, with all your
soul, with all your mind, and with all your strength.*

—MARK 12:30

Most of us have, at one time or another, drawn back from a
commitment that would require more than a few hours'
time and energy. Our main role models for total
involvement are star athletes and obsessed artists. And
when a religious person gives his or her all to God, that
person is labeled a fanatic. Are we willing even to explore
what it means to love with everything we have?

Hosea 14:2–10
Psalm 81
Mark 12:28–34

⋺ 98 ⋵

MARCH 5

Come, let us return to the LORD,
For it is he who has rent, but he will heal us;
he has struck us, but he will bind our wounds.

—HOSEA 6:1

Stacey knew that sooner or later she would have to face her mom again. Her mom had given her an extended time-out for behaving badly. But her mom would also be the one to forgive her and give her hugs, to cook her dinner and make her feel safe and comfy at bedtime. So when the time-out was over, Stacey went first to the one who always loved her.

Hosea 6:1–6
Psalm 51
Luke 18:9–14

The LORD is my shepherd;
there is nothing I lack.
In green pastures you let me graze;
to safe waters you lead me;
you restore my strength.
—PSALM 23:1–3

I grew up in the country, and I know that a good farmer makes sure his animals are fed and sheltered. In winter he breaks up ice on the pond so they can drink. And in the spring he watches for the new calves to be born, assisting when necessary. The ongoing care of the good farmer (or good shepherd), helps me recognize how tenderhearted Jesus is toward me, day after day.

1 Samuel 16:1, 6–7, 10–13
Psalm 23
Ephesians 5:8–14
John 9:1–41 or 9:1, 6–9, 13–17, 34–38

You changed my mourning into dancing;
you took off my sackcloth
and clothed me with gladness.

—PSALM 30:12

Jason had been in mourning for most of his life, for real and imagined losses. He wore his sorrow like clothing. Then a friend challenged him to read just one short passage of the Bible every day for a year. Slowly, Jason's outlook shifted as he discovered that love and celebration were just as real as pain and grief. His outward circumstances didn't really change, but Jason learned to see a fuller vision of life with God.

Isaiah 65:17–21
Psalm 30
John 4:43–54

MARCH 8

The man went and told the Jews that Jesus was the one who had made him well. Therefore, the Jews began to persecute Jesus because he did this on a sabbath.

—JOHN 5:15–16

After he was converted, John's behavior was so radically different that some people thought he was crazy. He went on to found a hospital where he could tend the sick. This was the beginning of the Order of the Brothers Hospitallers, and "crazy" John became St. John of God.

Ezekiel 47:1–9, 12
Psalm 46
John 5:1–16

Can a mother forget her infant,
be without tenderness for the child of her womb?
Even should she forget,
I will never forget you.
—ISAIAH 49:15

We can't imagine a mother forgetting to feed her infant or being completely without tenderness for her child. A woman's natural response is to attend immediately to her child's every need. The prophet Isaiah uses this image to emphasize how fervently and tenderly God cares for us.

Isaiah 49:8–15
Psalm 145
John 5:17–30

MARCH 10

> But they soon forgot all he had done;
> they had no patience for his plan.
> In the desert they gave way to their cravings,
> tempted God in the wasteland.
>
> —PSALM 106:13–14

In the midst of his complaining, it occurred to Ted that a lot of things had worked out pretty well. He felt ashamed as he remembered the answered prayers of recent weeks. Yet here he was again, fuming about some inconvenience, some aspect of his life that wasn't just the way he wanted it. When he realized his own fickle behavior, he was even more grateful for God's patience.

Exodus 32:7–14
Psalm 106
John 5:31–47

MARCH 11

And they knew not the hidden counsels of God;
neither did they count on a recompense of holiness
nor discern the innocent souls' reward.

—WISDOM 2:22

Regardless of how the world appears, God's justice will
prevail in the end. This verse from the book of Wisdom is
a good one to repeat to ourselves when life is unfair. We
may not know God's ways, but we know God, who knows
all and takes care of the future.

Wisdom 2:1, 12–22
Psalm 34
John 7:1–2, 10, 25–30

Some in the crowd who heard these words said, "This is truly the Prophet." Others said, "This is the Messiah." But others said, "The Messiah will not come from Galilee, will he?"

—JOHN 7:40–41

The boy came from a welfare family that was looked down upon by most of the townspeople. Then one day the family's house caught fire, and it was little Eddy who carried his baby sister through the flames to safety. For his heroism he was flown to Washington, D.C., and given an award by the president of the United States. The townspeople cheered him for a while, but soon they forgot about it. Eddy was still from the wrong side of town; he was not the hero they wanted.

Jeremiah 11:18–20
Psalm 7
John 7:40–53

[Jesus] cried out in a loud voice, "Lazarus, come out!" The dead man came out, tied hand and foot with burial bands, and his face was wrapped in a cloth. So Jesus said to them, "Untie him and let him go."
—JOHN 11:43–44

Jesus raised Lazarus from the dead, but he did not untie his hands and feet. He left that task to Lazarus's friends and family. What a lesson in healing. Even when God does miraculous work in us, we need the love of community to make that work complete.

Ezekiel 37:12–14
Psalm 130
Romans 8:8–11
John 11:1–45 or 11:3–7, 17, 20–27, 33–45

MARCH 14

When the old men saw her enter every day for her walk, they began to lust for her. They suppressed their consciences; they would not allow their eyes to look to heaven, and did not keep in mind just judgments.

—DANIEL 13:8–9

Possibly the most telling phrase in this passage is "they suppressed their consciences." This is exactly what we do before doing something we know is wrong. We don't fall into sin unwittingly; we make choices all along the way. The key to avoiding sin is self-awareness.

Daniel 13:1–9, 15–17, 19–30, 33–62 or 13:41–62
Psalm 23
John 8:1–11

MARCH 15

Let this be written for the next generation,
for a people not yet born,
that they may praise the LORD:
"The LORD looked down from the holy heights,
viewed the earth from heaven,
To attend to the groaning of the prisoners,
to release those doomed to die."

—PSALM 102:19–21

Jewish writer and Holocaust survivor Elie Wiesel often tells audiences that we must never forget those who have suffered—and we must tell their stories. The psalmist, too, understood how important it is for our stories to be passed on. How can we preserve the stories of our own generation?

Numbers 21:4–9
Psalm 102
John 8:21–30

———————————

MARCH 16

King Nebuchadnezzar rose in haste and asked his nobles, "Did we not cast three men bound into the fire?" "Assuredly, O king," they answered. "But," he replied, "I see four men unfettered and unhurt, walking in the fire, and the fourth looks like a son of God."

—DANIEL 3:91–92

Almighty God, help us remember that there is always a "fourth" person walking with us—among the flames and the storms, the wars and the darkness. Your Son is with us, and because of this we will ultimately walk freely and unhurt.

Daniel 3:14–20, 91–92, 95
Daniel 3:52–56
John 8:31–42

So the Jews said to him, "You are not yet fifty years old and you have seen Abraham?" Jesus said to them, "Amen, amen, I say to you, before Abraham came to be, I AM."

—JOHN 8:57–58

It's impossible for us to understand the mysteries of time and eternity, but we get a clue from Jesus' words in this passage. He had existed before he was Jesus the human being. Is it possible that someday we, too, will not be subject to time's boundaries? At the very least, we can rest assured that God's love circumvents any law of nature in order to reach us.

Genesis 17:3–9
Psalm 105
John 8:51–59

Truly, who is God except the LORD?
Who but our God is the rock?
This God who girded me with might,
kept my way unerring.

—PSALM 18:32–33

St. Cyril, patriarch of Jerusalem, served half his time as bishop in exile. Yet he was a master teacher of the catechism, his instructions so highly regarded that he was made a doctor of the church. If God has work for you to do, you will be able to do it, regardless of the circumstances.

Jeremiah 20:10–13
Psalm 18
John 10:31–42

[T]he angel of the Lord appeared to him in a dream and said, "Joseph, son of David, do not be afraid to take Mary your wife into your home. For it is through the holy Spirit that this child has been conceived in her." . . . When Joseph awoke, he did as the angel of the Lord had commanded him and took his wife into his home.

—MATTHEW 1:20, 24

We probably don't celebrate Joseph enough. Like Mary, he needed a lot of faith to participate in this bizarre set of circumstances. He, too, had to say yes to God and do exactly as he was instructed. And he had to watch his wife grow heavy with a child that was not his. Today, remember the faith and obedience of Jesus' earthly father.

2 Samuel 7:4–5, 12–14, 16
Psalm 89
Romans 4:13, 16–18, 22
Matthew 1:16, 18–21, 24 or Luke 2:41–51

Sunday
MARCH 20

Then Jesus came with them to a place called Gethsemane, and he said to his disciples, "Sit here while I go over there and pray." He took along Peter and the two sons of Zebedee, and began to feel sorrow and distress. Then he said to them, "My soul is sorrowful even to death. Remain here and keep watch with me."

—MATTHEW 26:36–38

Lord Jesus, you are the Son of God, but you needed your very human friends during this dark hour. We are awed that you became such a vulnerable person in this world. In our greatest sorrow, remind us of your journey.

Matthew 21:1–11
Psalm 22
Isaiah 50:4–7
Philippians 2:6–11
Matthew 26:14–27:66 or 27:11–54

MARCH 21

Mary took a liter of costly perfumed oil made from genuine aromatic nard and anointed the feet of Jesus and dried them with her hair; the house was filled with the fragrance of the oil.

—JOHN 12:3

I love the detail that "the house was filled with the fragrance." We can be sure that Mary (and others in the house that day) never smelled that fragrance again without remembering Jesus' words and actions. Try to remember some physical sensation that accompanied an important moment in your spiritual growth. How does this affect your thinking about incense, candles, and other physical factors in prayer and worship?

Isaiah 42:1–7
Psalm 27
John 12:1–11

MARCH 22

Peter said to him, "Master, why can't I follow you now? I will lay down my life for you." Jesus answered, "Will you lay down your life for me? Amen, amen, I say to you, the cock will not crow before you deny me three times."

—JOHN 13:37–38

Have you ever considered that it's impossible for you to disappoint Jesus? He already knows your weaknesses. He foresees your mistakes before you see even the possibility of them. Rather than worry about Jesus' reaction to your missteps, why not trust more readily in his patience and forgiveness?

Isaiah 49:1–6
Psalm 71
John 13:21–33, 36–38

The Lord GOD has given me
a well-trained tongue,
That I might know how to speak to the weary
a word that will rouse them.
Morning after morning
he opens my ear that I may hear,
And I have not rebelled,
have not turned back.
—ISAIAH 50:4–5

Each of us struggles sometimes to know the right words to say, especially to those who are weary or grief stricken. But the Lord has given us a well-trained tongue. If we are careful to listen, "morning after morning," God will give us wisdom and all the words we need.

Isaiah 50:4–9
Psalm 69
Matthew 26:14–25

*Then he poured water into a basin and began to wash the disciples' feet
and dry them with the towel around his waist. . . . "What I am doing,
you do not understand now, but you will understand later."*

—JOHN 13:5, 7

Jesus knew that his time on earth was coming to a close. It
was his last night with the disciples. So what did he do?
Summarize his teachings? Give instructions on how to deal
with the Romans and religious leaders? Give the disciples
messages to pass on to his family? No, the great rabbi
washed his disciples' dirty feet. He knew that this act of love
and service would speak to them—and to us—for centuries.

Chrism Mass:	Lord's Supper:
Isaiah 61:1–3, 6, 8–9	Exodus 12:1–8, 11–14
Psalm 89	Psalm 116
Revelation 1:5–8	1 Corinthians 11:23–26
Luke 4:16–21	John 13:1–15

For we do not have a high priest who is unable to sympathize with our weaknesses, but one who has similarly been tested in every way, yet without sin. So let us confidently approach the throne of grace to receive mercy and to find grace for timely help.

—HEBREWS 4:15–16

In one cell of the prison, the inmates had painted a mural depicting Jesus on the cross. They explained, "He's doing time for the rest of us." Because Jesus has suffered, any one of us can turn to him now to find the help we need, even in agonizing circumstances.

Isaiah 52:13–53:12
Psalm 31
Hebrews 4:14–16; 5:7–9
John 18:1–19:42

Early the next morning Abraham saddled his donkey, took with him his son Isaac, and two of his servants as well, and with the wood that he had cut for the holocaust, set out for the place of which God had told him.

—GENESIS 22:3

Abraham was on his way to sacrifice his son as a burnt offering to God. The journey took three days. Can you imagine how agonizing that was for Abraham, who knew what he must do and wondered what God would do? On Holy Saturday we remember the painful waiting of Jesus' disciples during the three days between his death and resurrection. We know the end of Abraham's story, and we know that Jesus indeed rose from the dead. We owe God our thanks for these tremendous stories that bolster our faith when all is dark.

Genesis 1:1–2:2 or 1:1, 26–31
Psalm 104 or 33
Genesis 22:1–18 or 22:1–2, 9–13, 15–18
Psalm 16
Exodus 14:15–15:1
Exodus 15:1–6, 17–18
Isaiah 54:5–14
Psalm 30
Isaiah 55:1–11
Isaiah 12:2–6
Baruch 3:9–15, 32–4:4
Psalm 19
Ezekiel 36:16–28
Psalms 42; 43 or Psalm 51
Romans 6:3–11
Psalm 118
Matthew 28:1–10

This man God raised [on] the third day and granted that he be visible, not to all the people, but to us, the witnesses chosen by God in advance, who ate and drank with him after he rose from the dead. . . . To him all the prophets bear witness, that everyone who believes in him will receive forgiveness of sins through his name.

—ACTS 10:40–41, 43

The Resurrection has become such an important religious celebration that we forget how weird the events actually were. It is a ghost story, but not really. The ghost had a body that could eat and drink. Jesus came back from the dead as a whole person. And because we believe in him, our lives will become more whole after death than they are now.

Acts 10:34, 37–43
Psalm 118
Colossians 3:1–4 or 1 Corinthians 5:6–8
John 20:1–9 or Matthew 28:1–10 or, at afternoon or evening Mass, Luke 24:13–35

MARCH 28

LORD, my allotted portion and my cup,
you have made my destiny secure.
Pleasant places were measured out for me;
fair to me indeed is my inheritance.

—PSALM 16:5–6

God has given you an inheritance of sorts. Your history,
your gifts, your opportunities, and your personal traits can
be considered your "portion" in life. Although some of that
inheritance may be difficult to accept (such as painful
events or family problems), you can begin to live out your
destiny only after you acknowledge what is yours and
choose to work with it.

Acts 2:14, 22–33
Psalm 16
Matthew 28:8–15

MARCH 29

And they said to her, "Woman, why are you weeping?" She said to them, "They have taken my Lord, and I don't know where they laid him." When she had said this, she turned around and saw Jesus there, but did not know it was Jesus.

—JOHN 20:13–14

Mary Magdalene went to Jesus' tomb expecting to find a corpse, not a risen Lord. Little wonder that she did not recognize Jesus at first. How many times and in how many places has Jesus been waiting to meet us, yet we were unable to see him because of our grief, confusion, or preconceived notions? Today, why not expect to see the One who is risen and who will be with us always?

Acts 2:36–41
Psalm 33
John 20:11–18

Wednesday

MARCH 30

They asked and he brought them quail;
with bread from heaven he filled them.
He split the rock and water gushed forth;
it flowed through the desert like a river.

—PSALM 105:40–41

He didn't know how he would feed his family, and then out
of nowhere he was offered a job that paid more than the
one he'd just lost. She was certain that her mother would
die from the illness, yet the woman rallied unexpectedly
and within days was released from the hospital. Do we dare
call these events miracles? Perhaps not, but we can certainly
attribute them to God's care for us.

Acts 3:1–10
Psalm 105
Luke 24:13–35

Then he opened their minds to understand the scriptures. And he said to them, "Thus it is written that the Messiah would suffer and rise from the dead on the third day and that repentance, for the forgiveness of sins, would be preached in his name to all the nations, beginning from Jerusalem."

—LUKE 24:45–47

She had heard Bible verses all her life, although she'd stopped going to church during her teens. Then one day she picked up a little book of Bible readings, and it was as if she had never seen those particular words before. They were exactly what she needed to help her face the difficulties in her life. Words by themselves do nothing, but when God opens a person's mind and heart, a single phrase can change a life.

Acts 3:11–26
Psalm 8
Luke 24:35–48

APRIL 1

Simon Peter said to them, "I am going fishing." They said to him, "We also will come with you." So they went out and got into the boat, but that night they caught nothing.

—JOHN 21:3

There's real humor in this passage. Jesus had died, risen from the dead, and even appeared to the disciples. But he was no longer with them as he had been. Peter actually thought he could go back to the life he'd had before he met Jesus. But once God has entered your life, you are forever changed. Faith will not always take you to comfortable places, but God will be with you in those places.

Acts 4:1–12
Psalm 118
John 21:1–14

[L]ater, as the eleven were at table, he appeared to them and rebuked them for their unbelief and hardness of heart because they had not believed those who saw him after he had been raised.

—MARK 16:14

Have you ever had to work to gain someone's trust? Do you remember how frustrating it was to explain to him again and again why he should believe you or do as you asked or stop worrying? Imagine Jesus' frustration at the unbelief of even his closest friends. Like those disciples, we, too, come to points when we must simply believe what is put before us and let go of speculation, doubt, cynicism, and fear.

Acts 4:13–21
Psalm 118
Mark 16:9–15

Now Jesus did many other signs in the presence of [his] disciples that are not written in this book. But these are written that you may [come to] believe that Jesus is the Messiah, the Son of God, and that through this belief you may have life in his name.

—JOHN 20:30–31

The apostle John is saying, in essence, "You don't know the half of it." Behind the written Scriptures are many unwritten stories about God's work in the world. And behind the mundane events in our lives are many works of the Holy Spirit, who constantly operates behind the scenes, unperceived by us.

Acts 2:42–47
Psalm 118
1 Peter 1:3–9
John 20:19–31

In the sixth month, the angel Gabriel was sent from God to a town of Galilee called Nazareth, to a virgin betrothed to a man named Joseph, of the house of David, and the virgin's name was Mary.

—LUKE 1:26–27

Not "once upon a time" but "in the sixth month." Not "in a place far away" but in "a town of Galilee called Nazareth." Luke recorded the specifics of the event that began the drama of the Incarnation. It was so unbelievable that God sent the angel Gabriel to explain to Mary what would happen. And then God inspired the Gospel writers to pass on this amazing story to us.

Isaiah 7:10–14; 8:10
Psalm 40
Hebrews 10:4–10
Luke 1:26–38

*The community of believers was of one heart and mind, and no one
claimed that any of his possessions was his own, but they had
everything in common.*

—ACTS 4:32

When Vincent Ferrer, a Dominican priest, was wandering
Europe in the fifteenth century, the church was in the midst
of a great schism. Vincent preached penance and performed
miracles as he traveled, hoping to heal the rift between
different parties of believers. No doubt he turned to this
passage in Acts. It is a passage we would do well to return
to now, when issues divide Christians across many lines.

Acts 4:32–37
Psalm 93
John 3:7–15

For God so loved the world that he gave his only Son, so that everyone who believes in him might not perish but might have eternal life.

—JOHN 3:16

We will never be able to explain this verse completely, but we can certainly appreciate it at face value. God didn't just send messages to our wounded world—God sent "his only Son," a part of God's very self, to save creation from destruction. God does not stand apart from us and merely observe; God is intimately involved with us through the life of Jesus.

Acts 5:17–26
Psalm 34
John 3:16–21

The LORD is close to the brokenhearted,
saves those whose spirit is crushed.
—PSALM 34:19

This psalm describes the people we like to stay away from—the woman so overwhelmed that her whole life is in chaos, the man so damaged that he's in counseling and on medications and still needy around his friends. "Those whose spirit is crushed" wander among us ignored and lonely because their desperation frightens us. May God give us the courage to love them as God does.

Acts 5:27–33
Psalm 34
John 3:31–36

[I]f this endeavor or this activity is of human origin, it will destroy itself. But if it comes from God, you will not be able to destroy them; you may even find yourselves fighting against God.

—ACTS 5:38–39

Therese wondered if her adolescent daughter's sudden enthusiasm for church could be trusted. Lisa was more involved with her faith than ever before, but would it pass, just like her admiration for the latest pop star? Therese's pastor eased her mind when he said, "What God does in a person's heart will last and help stabilize everything else." So Therese turned her worry into prayer, asking God to form true, lasting faith in Lisa.

Acts 5:34–42
Psalm 27
John 6:1–15

Let all the earth fear the LORD;
let all who dwell in the world show reverence.
For he spoke, and it came to be,
commanded, and it stood in place.
—PSALM 33:8–9

I owe to God my existence, the earth on which I live, and
the breath that keeps me going. What other reason do I
need to give God reverence? Every aspect of my life holds
together because God has chosen to let it be so. I risk
forgetting this, so at least once every day I acknowledge
that God spoke my life into being and sustains it moment
by moment.

Acts 6:1–7
Psalm 33
John 6:16–21

He was known before the foundation of the world but revealed in the final time for you, who through him believe in God who raised him from the dead and gave him glory, so that your faith and hope are in God.

—1 PETER 1:20–21

When Jesus came into the world, humanity was given access to a great secret. God's very self was revealed to us, not through magic or theory but through a person. That person not only lived but died and then lived again, and thus another cosmic secret was revealed: there is more to life than what we now see. There is something "on the other side," and we are part of that.

Acts 2:14, 22–33
Psalm 16
1 Peter 1:17–21
Luke 24:13–35

APRIL 11

• SAINT STANISLAUS, BISHOP AND MARTYR •

Your laws become my songs
wherever I make my home.
—PSALM 119:54

The day had been full of trouble, and her emotions had worn thin. During it all, she'd been trying to get a tune out of her head, a song she'd learned decades ago in Sunday school. Perhaps, she decided, a Top 40 hit about being sexy just would not help today. So she gave in to memory and sang the familiar words softly: "Jesus loves me, this I know . . ."

Acts 6:8–15
Psalm 119
John 6:22–29

APRIL 12

Which of the prophets did your ancestors not persecute? They put to death those who foretold the coming of the righteous one, whose betrayers and murderers you have now become. You received the law as transmitted by angels, but you did not observe it.

—ACTS 7:52–53

This passage is a warning for all of us. We are receiving word from God all the time—through events, through people, in any way imaginable. But if our hearts are not prepared for God, an angel might hand us a message and we wouldn't even know it.

Acts 7:51–8:1
Psalm 31
John 6:30–35

On that day, there broke out a severe persecution of the church in
Jerusalem, and all were scattered throughout the countryside of Judea
and Samaria, except the apostles. . . . Now those who had been
scattered went about preaching the word.

—ACTS 8:1, 4

Persecution may scatter God's people, but it usually spreads
the Good News. Ever since the first believers were forced
to leave Jerusalem, the faithful have carried the gospel to
every place they went. Today believers continue to
proclaim the Christian message in hostile, even dangerous,
environments. Pray for those who suffer for their faith, that
they won't give up hope.

Acts 8:1–8
Psalm 66
John 6:35–40

I am the bread of life. Your ancestors ate the manna in the desert, but they died; this is the bread that comes down from heaven so that one may eat it and not die.

—JOHN 6:48–50

I once saved a baby bird that I found in some shrubbery. I managed to feed it mashed chick feed. What I didn't know was that baby birds must be fed almost constantly. I went to bed, intending to feed it when I woke up. But a few missed feedings during the night were enough to kill the chick. It's easy to see how a small creature requires nourishment to live. But I rarely think about how I need to be nourished by God's love and wisdom in order to stay spiritually vital.

Acts 8:26–40
Psalm 66
John 6:44–51

APRIL 15

Saul got up from the ground, but when he opened his eyes he could see nothing; so they led him by the hand and brought him to Damascus. For three days he was unable to see, and he neither ate nor drank.

—ACTS 9:8–9

Saul was blinded by a strange light. What happened to you? What wake-up call did you receive, or what experience stopped you cold and made you examine your life? Are you due for another such event, or have you continued to pay attention to what is important?

Acts 9:1–20
Psalm 117
John 6:52–59

Jesus then said to the Twelve, "Do you also want to leave?" Simon Peter answered him, "Master, to whom shall we go? You have the words of eternal life."

—JOHN 6:67–68

Most of us come to this point. We aren't particularly pleased with our faith or our church or our life in general. But we have to ask, "Where else do I go? What else can I do?" Simon Peter recognized that the life of faith would be difficult, and already many people had stopped following Jesus. But this life was the true life, and there was no substitute.

Acts 9:31–42
Psalm 116
John 6:60–69

Sunday

APRIL 17

He himself bore our sins in his body upon the cross, so that, free from sin, we might live for righteousness. By his wounds you have been healed.

—1 PETER 2:24

Sin has damaged me. I am wounded by my own wrongdoing and by the wrongdoing of others. In a mysterious way, Christ's suffering and death can heal that damage. How might my life change if I ask God in prayer to heal the results of my selfishness or my resentment?

Acts 2:14, 36–41
Psalm 23
1 Peter 2:20–25
John 10:1–10

I have other sheep that do not belong to this fold. These also I must lead, and they will hear my voice, and there will be one flock, one shepherd.

—JOHN 10:16

Jesus tells us here that many people belong to God's family, and we won't always know who they are. All the more reason to treat every person as if he or she is a brother or sister.

Acts 11:1–18
Psalm 42
John 10:11–18

APRIL 19

My sheep hear my voice; I know them, and they follow me. I give them eternal life, and they shall never perish. No one can take them out of my hand.

—JOHN 10:27–28

Can you remember a time when you were a child and were stuck up in a tree or on a fence? Down below your mom or dad or an older kid called out to you, "Just let go—I'll catch you!" There was that moment of falling when you weren't really sure—and then suddenly you were caught in strong arms, and you'd never felt safer. Every day Jesus says to us, "Don't be afraid—I'll catch you!"

Acts 11:19–26
Psalm 87
John 10:22–30

*While they were worshiping the Lord and fasting, the holy Spirit said,
"Set apart for me Barnabas and Saul for the work to which I have
called them." Then, completing their fasting and prayer, they laid hands
on them and sent them off.*

—ACTS 13:2–3

Anyone who has received a calling can describe the
moment it became clear and unmistakable. What moment
or moments in your life have convinced you of what you
needed to do? Are you being called to do something at this
moment?

Acts 12:24–13:5
Psalm 67
John 12:44–50

Where are your promises of old, Lord,
the loyalty sworn to David?
Remember, Lord, the insults to your servants,
how I bear all the slanders of the nations.
Your enemies, LORD, insult your anointed;
they insult my every endeavor.

—PSALM 89:50–52

Sometimes people feel inclined to "protect" God's reputation by denying life's harsher realities. But, in fact, there are times when we are assaulted on every side and our endeavors are thwarted at every turn. Like the psalmist, we must be brutally honest when we pray. It is the only way to move forward.

Acts 13:13–25
Psalm 89
John 13:16–20

In my Father's house there are many dwelling places. If there were not, would I have told you that I am going to prepare a place for you? And if I go and prepare a place for you, I will come back again and take you to myself, so that where I am you also may be.

—JOHN 14:2–3

A hospice chaplain, Ron is convinced that something awaits us on the other side of death. He has watched many people die so certain that they were on a journey and that they were not alone. Jesus was very straightforward about this topic: he has gone ahead to prepare a place for us so that we will always be with him.

Acts 13:26–33
Psalm 2
John 14:1–6

Philip said to him, "Master, show us the Father, and that will be enough for us." Jesus said to him, "Have I been with you for so long a time and you still do not know me, Philip? Whoever has seen me has seen the Father."

—JOHN 14:8–9

Philip wanted to see God, but maybe Jesus was a little too real for him—a human being who spoke plainly and gave him work to do. What might Philip have been looking for? What do we really look for when we seek God?

Acts 13:44–52
Psalm 98
John 14:7–14

[T]he LORD's word is true;
all his works are trustworthy.
The LORD loves justice and right
and fills the earth with goodness.

—PSALM 33:4–5

Yes, Lord, we really can trust you. We can rely on your goodness and fairness. We can't trust governments or powerful people or even our own family members at times. But your truth is forever.

Acts 6:1–7
Psalm 33
1 Peter 2:4–9
John 14:1–12

Monday

APRIL 25

• SAINT MARK, EVANGELIST •

The God of all grace who called you to his eternal glory through Christ [Jesus] will himself restore, confirm, strengthen, and establish you after you have suffered a little.

—1 PETER 5:10

God has called us to this life in Christ. God watches over us as we struggle and knows our suffering. And God will restore us when the suffering is done. We may feel that our success or failure depends on our own strength and perseverance. But God initiated this faith journey, and God will help us complete it.

1 Peter 5:5–14
Psalm 89
Mark 16:15–20

APRIL 26

Peace I leave with you; my peace I give to you. Not as the world gives do I give it to you. Do not let your hearts be troubled or afraid.

—JOHN 14:27

Jesus recognized how frightened his disciples were. He understood that the idea of his own death and resurrection and the spiritual transformations that were taking place within his followers were all disturbing to some degree. Even good change is scary. Rather than be surprised or upset about our fear, we can simply take Jesus' words to heart.

Acts 14:19–28
Psalm 145
John 14:27–31

I am the vine, you are the branches. Whoever remains in me and I in him will bear much fruit, because without me you can do nothing.
—JOHN 15:5

I once heard someone say that a Christian's life should not be explainable apart from supernatural grace and wisdom. What we strive to do is not really possible without the power of Christ. So there is such a thing as healthy dependence. Through our continuing fellowship with Jesus we are given everything we need. This is why prayer and faith are so essential to the Christian life.

Acts 15:1–6
Psalm 122
John 15:1–8

APRIL 28

He made no distinction between us and them, for by faith he purified their hearts. Why, then, are you now putting God to the test by placing on the shoulders of the disciples a yoke that neither our ancestors nor we have been able to bear?

—ACTS 15:9–10

Peter was addressing Jewish Christians who wanted to make gentile believers follow Jewish religious law. After Peter spoke, the church decided not to place the burden of an unfamiliar religious culture on new believers. Christian missionaries have not always followed the apostles' example, and still today we must be sensitive to people who come to the faith. We can begin by asking, "What is truly necessary to faith, and what is merely cultural or customary?"

Acts 15:7–21
Psalm 96
John 15:9–11

My heart is steadfast, God,
my heart is steadfast.
I will sing and chant praise.
—PSALM 57:8

Singing and chanting have been part of daily religious life for centuries, but you don't have to be in a religious order to develop this habit. Today, try singing a simple song of praise for God that might help your heart stay focused on the One who is good.

Acts 15:22–31
Psalm 57
John 15:12–17

Saturday

APRIL 30

• SAINT PIUS V, POPE •

*During [the] night Paul had a vision. A Macedonian stood before
him and implored him with these words, "Come over to Macedonia
and help us." When he had seen the vision, we sought passage to
Macedonia at once, concluding that God had called us to proclaim
the good news to them.*

—ACTS 16:9–10

Paul and his companions trusted God to work through any
means possible to give them direction. How has God
spoken to you? It's very likely that God has used a variety
of things to communicate with you: dreams, hunches,
circumstances, people, and Scripture, to name a few. How
can you be more open to signals from God?

Acts 16:1–10
Psalm 100
John 15:18–21

Always be ready to give an explanation to anyone who asks you for a reason for your hope, but do it with gentleness and reverence, keeping your conscience clear, so that, when you are maligned, those who defame your good conduct in Christ may themselves be put to shame.

—1 PETER 3:15–16

First, the guys were curious when Thomas didn't react to their insults. Then they were suspicious when they asked him about it and he said something about dignity. But what won them over was how totally unhostile he remained, even as they questioned him and tried to find fault with his explanations. They couldn't argue with the graciousness of his spirit; they could only leave him alone—or become his friends.

Acts 8:5–8, 14–17
Psalm 66
1 Peter 3:15–18
John 14:15–21

Monday

MAY 2

When the Advocate comes whom I will send you from the Father, the Spirit of truth that proceeds from the Father, he will testify to me.

—JOHN 15:26

Holy Spirit, Advocate, I need your truth today more than ever. Everyone has a different version of "the truth"; if you don't lead me, I can't be confident of my next step. May I always be open to your work in my life.

Acts 16:11–15
Psalm 149
John 15:26–16:4

───────────

Tuesday

MAY 3

• SAINTS JAMES AND PHILIP, APOSTLES •

Let the words of my mouth meet with your favor,
keep the thoughts of my heart before you,
LORD, my rock and my redeemer.

—PSALM 19:15

This short prayer is especially fitting for a person who works with words—author, speaker, or teacher. One writer I know begins each day's work by praying this verse or some version of it. As you go through the day, no matter what your profession, dedicate the words of your mouth and the thoughts of your heart to God.

1 Corinthians 15:1–8
Psalm 19
John 14:6–14

*[God] made from one the whole human race to dwell on the entire
surface of the earth, and he fixed the ordered seasons and the boundaries
of their regions, so that people might seek God, even perhaps grope for
him and find him, though indeed he is not far from any one of us.*

—ACTS 17:26–27

The missionary came across an old Korean man sitting on a
bench. They began to chat, and when the old man asked the
missionary about his work, he explained that he told the
world about God's Son, Jesus. The old man's face lit up. He
said, "Jesus—yes! I have known for a long time that God had
a Son, and I have waited all this time to learn his name."

Acts 17:15, 22–18:1
Psalm 148
John 16:12–15

"[Y]ou will receive power when the holy Spirit comes upon you, and you will be my witnesses in Jerusalem, throughout Judea and Samaria, and to the ends of the earth." When he had said this, as they were looking on, he was lifted up, and a cloud took him from their sight.

—ACTS 1:8–9

It was Matt's first day as a college instructor. The night before, he'd had dinner with his mentor, a professor who was now retired. At the end of the night, when his friend said good-bye, got into his car, and drove away, Matt had never felt so alone. But now, as he stood before twenty new faces, he imagined his mentor standing in the back of the room, smiling at him. *I was trained by the best,* Matt thought. *I'm not really alone.*

Acts 1:1–11
Psalm 47
Ephesians 1:17–23
Matthew 28:16–20

Friday

MAY 6

Amen, amen, I say to you, you will weep and mourn, while the world rejoices; you will grieve, but your grief will become joy.

—JOHN 16:20

Diane discovered that she could not experience true conversion of spirit until she had faced her life—all of it—and grieved the wrong she had done to others and the wrong others had done to her. She'd always thought that faith was what weak people turned to in order to escape life. But faith now required complete honesty, and only after that did the joy come.

Acts 18:9–18
Psalm 47
John 16:20–23

⇒ 162 ⇐

Saturday

MAY 7

I came from the Father and have come into the world. Now I am leaving the world and going back to the Father.

—JOHN 16:28

Jesus knew who he was. He knew where he came from and where he was going. Who are you? How did you get to where you are today? And where are you headed right now? Allow this little exercise to help you refocus and continue your day in confidence.

Acts 18:23–28
Psalm 47
John 16:23–28

God will hide me in his shelter
in time of trouble,
Will conceal me in the cover of his tent;
and set me high upon a rock.

—PSALM 27:5

Try to remember a time when you felt completely safe—
maybe in your mother's arms after a nightmare or snug in
your house during a thunderstorm. Spend a few moments
re-creating that feeling of security. Then bring that feeling
into your time of prayer. Imagine God holding you in
sheltering arms when you are frightened. Picture God's
love as a warm, quiet place safe from the danger that roams
just outside the door.

Acts 1:12–14
Psalm 27
1 Peter 4:13–16
John 17:1–11

Monday

MAY 9

I have told you this so that you might have peace in me. In the world you will have trouble, but take courage, I have conquered the world.

—JOHN 16:33

Tim was amazed at how calmly his mother accepted the news that she'd been laid off. Tim's dad was long gone, and now so was their only source of income. But his mom sighed and said, "God has never promised us we wouldn't have problems. We'll just have to trust that he's watching over us and will help us get through whatever happens."

Acts 19:1–8
Psalm 68
John 16:29–33

• BLESSED JOSEPH DE VEUSTER OF MOLOKA'I (FATHER DAMIEN), PRIEST •

But now, compelled by the Spirit, I am going to Jerusalem. What will happen to me there I do not know, except that in one city after another the holy Spirit has been warning me that imprisonment and hardships await me.

—ACTS 20:22–23

When Fr. Damien volunteered to work with the lepers on the Isle of Moloka'i, he knew that eventually he would become afflicted with the disease. But God's love compelled him to work lovingly and passionately with these people whom no one else would even come near. Damien did contract leprosy and died at the age of forty-nine. He was buried among the other lepers of the colony.

Acts 20:17–27
Psalm 68
John 17:1–11

I do not ask that you take them out of the world but that you keep them from the evil one.

—JOHN 17:15

Jesus acknowledged that there is evil in this world, but he didn't ask God to gather all his followers and bring them out of the world and into heaven. It is important that we go through this earthly life. We have lessons to learn and work to do. We can look forward to heaven, but we were never meant to waste our energy longing after escape.

Acts 20:28–38
Psalm 68
John 17:11–19

I pray not only for them, but also for those who will believe in me through their word, so that they may all be one, as you, Father, are in me and I in you, that they also may be in us, that the world may believe that you sent me.

—JOHN 17:20–21

Jesus prays here for you and for me. When he asked God to give his believers unity, he included the people who would become his followers on the basis of the words of the disciples. Here's a spiritual exercise: Read all of John 17 and put your own name in every place where Jesus mentions his followers.

Acts 22:30; 23:6–11
Psalm 16
John 17:20–26

Friday

MAY 13

As the heavens tower over the earth,
so God's love towers over the faithful.
As far as the east is from the west,
so far have our sins been removed from us.
—PSALM 103:11–12

Bible scholar J. B. Phillips published a book years ago titled *Your God Is Too Small.* His premise was that we expect too little of God and that we in fact think of God as a slightly larger version of us—as the resident police officer or managing director. What images of God dominate your thinking? Do any of them make God small and inadequate?

Acts 25:13–21
Psalm 103
John 21:15–19

Then they prayed, "You, Lord, who know the hearts of all, show which one of these two you have chosen to take the place in this apostolic ministry from which Judas turned away to go to his own place." Then they gave lots to them, and the lot fell upon Matthias, and he was counted with the eleven apostles.

—ACTS 1:24–26

Karen had been with the agency for five years, doing everything from stuffing envelopes to approaching potential donors. Then the director of the agency died from a sudden massive stroke, and in one short meeting the board appointed Karen to take his place. They said, "You know the inner workings of this agency better than anyone." We never know when a door will open and years of uneventful work will provide the perfect credentials.

Acts 1:15–17, 20–26
Psalm 113
John 15:9–17

Sunday

MAY 15

• PENTECOST SUNDAY •

There are different kinds of spiritual gifts but the same Spirit; there are different forms of service but the same Lord; there are different workings but the same God who produces all of them in everyone. To each individual the manifestation of the Spirit is given for some benefit.

—1 CORINTHIANS 12:4–7

Because the Holy Spirit came to us, our lives are developed according to gifts rather than needs, cooperation rather than competition, and loving service rather than grasping domination. No wonder Christianity—in its truest expressions—is radical and world changing.

Vigil:
Genesis 11:1–9 or Exodus 19:3–8, 16–20 or
Ezekiel 37:1–14 or Joel 3:1–5
Psalm 104
Romans 8:22–27
John 7:37–39

Day:
Acts 2:1–11
Psalm 104
1 Corinthians 12:3–7, 12–13
John 20:19–23

All wisdom comes from the LORD
and with him it remains forever.
The sand of the seashore, the drops of rain,
the days of eternity: who can number these?
Heaven's height, earth's breadth,
the depths of the abyss: who can explore these?

—SIRACH 1:1–3

For every person who has turned to God after engaging in intensive theological seeking, there are probably several more who have turned to God after gazing at a starry sky or the Grand Canyon. In fact, nature is a good antidote to a fretful soul. When you need perspective or simply rest, spend a few moments taking in "heaven's height, earth's breadth."

Sirach 1:1–10
Psalm 93
Mark 9:14–29

Give up your anger, abandon your wrath;
do not be provoked; it brings only harm.

—PSALM 37:8

She went to the antiwar rally because she wanted peaceful solutions to international problems. Many who walked with her also wanted peace. But in the large crowd were others whose anger seemed at odds with the whole point of the demonstration. And it was that anger that later helped turn a peaceful demonstration into a riot. The biblical writer understood the damaging effects of wrath, and the words of this psalm are as true today as ever.

Sirach 2:1–11
Psalm 37
Mark 9:30–37

"Teacher, we saw someone driving out demons in your name, and we tried to prevent him because he does not follow us." Jesus replied, "Do not prevent him. . . . For whoever is not against us is for us."

—MARK 9:38–40

What would the church be like if all of us followed this simple advice? Christendom is full of groups and subgroups and splinter groups, many of them fighting with or bad-mouthing one another. Why are we so suspicious of people who don't "follow us"? "Do not prevent them," Jesus said. May we stop getting in the way of the work God is accomplishing through others.

Sirach 4:11–19
Psalm 119
Mark 9:38–40

And if your eye causes you to sin, pluck it out. Better for you to enter into the kingdom of God with one eye than with two eyes to be thrown into Gehenna.

—MARK 9:47

Alan decided he had to give up some of his video games. They were consuming more and more of his time, and as much as he enjoyed the challenge and the strategizing, he noticed that he stayed in play/war mode even when he was doing other things. He began to feel as if he didn't control his own thoughts and emotions anymore. He decided that freedom had a higher value than entertainment.

Sirach 5:1–8
Psalm 1
Mark 9:41–50

Friday

MAY 20

• SAINT BERNARDINE OF SIENA, PRIEST •

Let your acquaintances be many,
but one in a thousand your confidant.
When you gain a friend, first test him,
and be not too ready to trust him.

—SIRACH 6:6–7

I used to think that every friendship had to become "close,"
and I worried about those friendships that remained
"superficial." But the years have taught me that there are
many levels of friendship. Sirach's author knew that only a
few people in one's life will become confidants. When we
realize this, we can take the pressure off ourselves and,
rather than try to make every relationship a major
friendship, appreciate each for what it is.

Sirach 6:5–17
Psalm 119
Mark 10:1–12

Saturday
MAY 21

• SAINT CHRISTOPHER MAGALLANES, PRIEST AND MARTYR, AND HIS
COMPANIONS, MARTYRS •

*And people were bringing children to him that he might touch them, but
the disciples rebuked them. When Jesus saw this he became indignant
and said to them, "Let the children come to me; do not prevent them, for
the kingdom of God belongs to such as these."*

—MARK 10:13–14

Sr. Marlene Halpin has worked with children for years, and
she says that contemplative prayer comes to them
naturally. They have not yet outgrown their sense of God's
presence, and the adult world hasn't yet dimmed their
spiritual vision. We should do all we can to protect the
spirituality of the children in our lives. The first step might
be to simply listen to them more attentively.

Sirach 17:1–15
Psalm 103
Mark 10:13–16

Sunday

MAY 22

Finally, brothers, rejoice. Mend your ways, encourage one another, agree with one another, live in peace, and the God of love and peace will be with you. Greet one another with a holy kiss. All the holy ones greet you.

—2 CORINTHIANS 13:11–12

During Sunday Mass, Ann looked around at the crowd. *What am I doing here?* she wondered. *What do I really have in common with these people?* Then the priest made the sign of the cross "in the name of the Father, and of the Son, and of the Holy Spirit," and Ann sensed that she had just come home. *We have God in common. And that's enough.*

Exodus 34:4–6, 8–9
Daniel 3:52–55
2 Corinthians 13:11–13
John 3:16–18

⇒ 178 ⇐

Monday

MAY 23

Jesus looked around and said to his disciples, "How hard it is for those who have wealth to enter the kingdom of God!"

—MARK 10:23

Before Jim and I got married, we had a frank discussion about what each of us valued. We agreed that it was important to do what each of us was gifted to do, even if that meant never making a lot of money. Twelve years later, we are still working with our gifts, and we don't have much money. But life is full of good things.

Sirach 17:20–24
Psalm 32
Mark 10:17–27

Give to the Most High as he has given to you,
generously, according to your means.
—SIRACH 35:9

"According to your means" is a crucial phrase in this passage from Sirach. Each of us must consider for ourselves what it means. Many times we are able to give more than we think, but at other times it's appropriate to give a smaller amount (of money, resources, or time) because of other pressing needs. The beauty of this principle is that it is as dynamic as life itself, and it encourages us to give "to the Most High"—to focus above all on our relationship with God.

Sirach 35:1–12
Psalm 50
Mark 10:28–31

Wednesday

MAY 25

• SAINT BEDE THE VENERABLE, PRIEST AND DOCTOR OF THE CHURCH •
SAINT GREGORY VII, POPE • SAINT MARY MAGDALENE DE' PAZZI, VIRGIN •

O God, the nations have invaded your heritage;
they have defiled your holy temple,
have laid Jerusalem in ruins. . . .
They have spilled their blood like water
all around Jerusalem,
and no one is left to bury them.

—PSALM 79:1, 3

These verses could describe many wars and acts of terror throughout the world. The psalmist's words are just as true now as they were thousands of years ago. Let us take several opportunities today to remember victims of war and ask God's mercy and discernment for those who seek peace.

Sirach 36:1, 4–5, 10–17
Psalm 79
Mark 10:32–45

Thursday

MAY 26

• SAINT PHILIP NERI, PRIEST •

Jesus said to him . . . "What do you want me to do for you?" The blind man replied to him, "Master, I want to see."

—MARK 10:51

Why do you suppose Jesus asked this question when it was clear that the man was blind? Would a blind man want to stay blind? It might seem obvious that he wouldn't, but we've all known people who, though troubled, do not want to get better. If Jesus were to sit with you at this moment and ask, "What do you want me to do for you?" what would your honest answer be?

Sirach 42:15–25
Psalm 33
Mark 10:46–52

Friday

MAY 27

• SAINT AUGUSTINE OF CANTERBURY, BISHOP •

They came to Jerusalem, and on entering the temple area he began to drive out those selling and buying there. He overturned the tables of the money changers and the seats of those who were selling doves. He did not permit anyone to carry anything through the temple area.

—MARK 11:15–16

An evangelist was in town for the weekend, and out of curiosity Julia went to hear him speak. She entered the church to find tables full of the speaker's merchandise. He referred to these items numerous times during his presentation. This man made the Christian life sound like just another great deal. Julia wondered if he would offer God at a discount if people didn't respond readily enough. After half an hour, she left in disgust.

Sirach 44:1, 9–13
Psalm 149
Mark 11:11–26

In the short time I paid heed,
I met with great instruction.
Since in this way I have profited,
I will give my teacher grateful praise.
—SIRACH 51:16–17

Sarah still recalls the teacher who encouraged her to paint, way back in grammar school. Now Sarah's works are on exhibit in art galleries, but who knows if that would be the case if she hadn't spent one year in the care of an attentive teacher, or if she hadn't responded to that care? Every day we are surrounded by opportunity. We can only pay heed and see what happens.

Sirach 51:12–20
Psalm 19
Mark 11:27–33

Sunday

MAY 29

• THE MOST HOLY BODY AND BLOOD OF CHRIST •

The cup of blessing that we bless, is it not a participation in the blood of Christ? The bread that we break, is it not a participation in the body of Christ?

—1 CORINTHIANS 10:16

Over the course of their many pilgrimages, María and Michael have discovered that no matter where they are or what language is spoken there, when they participate in the Eucharist they are among brothers and sisters. The body and blood of Christ connect all of his followers in a mystical way, and those bonds are strong enough to transcend many differences.

Deuteronomy 8:2–3, 14–16
Psalm 147
1 Corinthians 10:16–17
John 6:51–58

All goes well for those gracious in lending,
who conduct their affairs with justice.
They shall never be shaken;
the just shall be remembered forever.
—PSALM 112:5–6

While the people who get the most media coverage are usually criminals, it is the just and generous who keep the world going and really deserve attention. Day in and day out, good people lend a hand, make the right decisions, and set holy examples for the rest of us. Ponder for a few moments today one or two people who fit the description in Psalm 112, and thank God for them.

Tobit 1:3; 2:1–8
Psalm 112
Mark 12:1–12

Rejoice with those who rejoice, weep with those who weep. Have the same regard for one another; do not be haughty but associate with the lowly; do not be wise in your own estimation.

—ROMANS 12:15–16

Rita had the ability to identify with everyone she met, regardless of the person's race, religion, livelihood, or economic status. She always found a way to uncover exactly what that person needed at that moment. Some people (who were likely jealous of her popularity) called her a chameleon. But most people saw her as someone who demonstrated Christian love at its finest.

Zephaniah 3:14–18 or Romans 12:9–16
Isaiah 12:2–6
Luke 1:39–56

Wednesday

JUNE 1

• SAINT JUSTIN, MARTYR •

Remember no more the sins of my youth;
remember me only in light of your love.
—PSALM 25:7

I can measure myself by all the wrong I've done, or I can
see myself simply as loved by God. But I can't take hold of
God's love if I am still hanging on to guilt and regret. God,
help me trust that your love will make up for all that I
cannot do or be.

Tobit 3:1–11, 16–17
Psalm 25
Mark 12:18–27

And when Jesus saw that [he] answered with understanding, he said to him, "You are not far from the kingdom of God." And no one dared to ask him any more questions.

—MARK 12:34

Imagine Jesus saying to you, "You are not far from the kingdom of God." What would you think that meant? What emotions would come over you? Would you be like the people who were around Jesus that day—afraid to ask more questions?

Tobit 6:10–11; 7:1, 9–17; 8:4–9
Psalm 128
Mark 12:28–34

*[Y]ou are a people sacred to the LORD, your God; he has chosen
you from all the nations on the face of the earth to be a people
peculiarly his own.*

—DEUTERONOMY 7:6

Paul was chosen to be a member of a team that would
travel to war-torn regions and facilitate reconciliation. As
part of this group, Paul saw himself in a new way: he was a
representative of peace. His life would be an example to
others, and his every word and gesture would be observed
closely. He was humbled by the responsibility yet eager for
the privilege. And he trusted that this new identity would
transform his own life.

Deuteronomy 7:6–11
Psalm 103
1 John 4:7–16
Matthew 11:25–30

Saturday

JUNE 4

• THE IMMACULATE HEART OF THE BLESSED VIRGIN MARY •

A king's secret it is prudent to keep, but the works of God are to be declared and made known. Praise them with due honor.
—TOBIT 12:7

The kids were mostly delinquents who had never been out of the city. When Keri led them to the canyon overlook, the toughest of them murmured a phrase that would normally be considered profane, but it was the only way he knew to express his awe over the massive rock formations, the shimmering river, and the autumn-covered slopes. Keri smiled, knowing that God the creator would recognize praise in any form.

Tobit 12:1, 5–15, 20
Tobit 13:2, 6
Luke 2:41–51

JUNE 5

He did not doubt God's promise in unbelief; rather, he was empowered by faith and gave glory to God and was fully convinced that what he had promised he was also able to do.

—ROMANS 4:20–21

Sometimes all we have to go on is deep conviction. We may not be able to explain our faith or even defend it very well. But we can trust God, who is trustworthy. We may fail, but God will do what God has promised. True faith rests upon our trust in God's character.

Hosea 6:3–6
Psalm 50
Romans 4:18–25
Matthew 9:9–13

Monday

JUNE 6

Blessed be the God and Father of our Lord Jesus Christ, the Father of compassion and God of all encouragement, who encourages us in our every affliction, so that we may be able to encourage those who are in any affliction with the encouragement with which we ourselves are encouraged by God.

—2 CORINTHIANS 1:3–4

It often seems that the people who can best comfort us are those who have suffered through what we're experiencing. Parents who have lost children to cancer, spouses of alcoholics, people who have been diagnosed with a rare disease—often they seek out, or are sought out by, people who share that specific pain. God designed us so that even in our grief and fatigue we can build up others. Who today might benefit from your encouragement?

2 Corinthians 1:1–7
Psalm 34
Matthew 5:1–12

But the one who gives us security with you in Christ and who anointed us is God; he has also put his seal upon us and given the Spirit in our hearts as a first installment.

—2 CORINTHIANS 1:21–22

Sometimes I wonder, *What if everything I believe is just a story?* And I'll argue with myself about my most basic beliefs. But at another level, my spirit is calm and my faith is secure. I can only explain this as God's Spirit within me communing with my spirit. This is a mystery, but I can be grateful for happenings inside me that make it possible for me to have true faith.

2 Corinthians 1:18–22
Psalm 119
Matthew 5:13–16

Do not think that I have come to abolish the law or the prophets. I have come not to abolish but to fulfill.

—MATTHEW 5:17

Jesus defied categorization. Radicals would have said, "The law is outdated—we're doing a new thing now." The establishment would have said, "The law is the law—it cannot be changed." But Jesus embraced the old while giving it new life. How can we bring this approach to our faith?

2 Corinthians 3:4–11
Psalm 99
Matthew 5:17–19

Thursday
JUNE 9

*[W]henever a person turns to the Lord the veil is removed. . . . All of us,
gazing with unveiled face on the glory of the Lord, are being
transformed into the same image from glory to glory, as from the Lord
who is the Spirit.*

—2 CORINTHIANS 3:16, 18

It has been observed that some married couples grow to
resemble each other physically over time. And children
often grow up not only to look very much like their
parents but also to speak, act, and think as their parents do.
This mirroring of others happens as we get to know them
well and as we learn to trust and love them. In the same
way, as we grow more deeply acquainted with God we will
become more like God in our character and outlook.

2 Corinthians 3:15–4:1, 3–6
Psalm 85
Matthew 5:20–26

We are afflicted in every way, but not constrained; perplexed, but not
driven to despair; persecuted, but not abandoned; struck down, but not
destroyed; always carrying about in the body the dying of Jesus, so
that the life of Jesus may also be manifested in our body.

—2 CORINTHIANS 4:8–10

The writer of these verses just kept going and going! How
does a person endure so much suffering while knowing that
it will only continue? The key is to believe that Jesus lives
through us, even in our tormented physical bodies.
Persecuted believers through the ages have thrived because
of this attitude. When we suffer, we can remind ourselves
that Jesus suffers with us.

2 Corinthians 4:7–15
Psalm 116
Matthew 5:27–32

When [Barnabas] arrived and saw the grace of God, he rejoiced and encouraged them all to remain faithful to the Lord in firmness of heart, for he was a good man, filled with the holy Spirit and faith. And a large number of people was added to the Lord.

—ACTS 11:23–24

You probably have a Barnabas in your life—a person whose very presence encourages you. Thank that person sometime soon. And ask yourself, "Who looks to me for courage and hope? How can I be a Barnabas to that person?"

Acts 11:21–26; 13:1–3
Psalm 98
Matthew 5:33–37

JUNE 12

Indeed, if, while we were enemies, we were reconciled to God through the death of his Son, how much more, once reconciled, will we be saved by his life.

—ROMANS 5:10

God is already on our side. The great gap between us and God exists mostly in our own thinking. The life, death, and resurrection of Christ took away the guilt we bore as a result of our sins and failings, and God already sees us as his own. If we truly believed this, how differently would we live?

Exodus 19:2–6
Psalm 100
Romans 5:6–11
Matthew 9:36–10:8

Working together, then, we appeal to you not to receive the grace of God in vain. . . . Behold, now is a very acceptable time; behold, now is the day of salvation.

—2 CORINTHIANS 6:1–2

Elizabeth kept telling herself that she would respond to that nagging in her soul. She felt the need to be quiet more, to explore prayer, and to find friends who would create a better atmosphere in her life. But it was easier to just keep going, day after day. Before she knew it, twenty years had gone by, and that bit of desire she'd once known had all but disappeared.

2 Corinthians 6:1–10
Psalm 98
Matthew 5:38–42

I say to you, love your enemies, and pray for those who persecute you, that you may be children of your heavenly Father, for he makes his sun rise on the bad and the good, and causes rain to fall on the just and the unjust.

—MATTHEW 5:44–45

I say that I want justice, but often what I really want is vengeance. I want people to get what they deserve, especially if they have harmed me. How far my thoughts have moved from this very basic teaching of Jesus! I should long for every person to receive blessings, and I should pray that the most irritating people find good in their lives.

2 Corinthians 8:1–9
Psalm 146
Matthew 5:43–48

Moreover, God is able to make every grace abundant for you, so that in all things, always having all you need, you may have an abundance for every good work.

—2 CORINTHIANS 9:8

The group of volunteers converged upon the neighborhood and began targeting homes that needed repairs, especially homes belonging to the elderly. They worked steadily for two weeks, sleeping on the church floors, eating cold cereal and baloney sandwiches, and sharing bathrooms. A local newspaper reporter asked one worker what it was like dealing with such conditions. "It's great," the man replied with a grin. "We have everything we need."

2 Corinthians 9:6–11
Psalm 112
Matthew 6:1–6, 16–18

Thursday

JUNE 16

Majestic and glorious is your work,
your wise design endures forever.
You won renown for your wondrous deeds;
gracious and merciful is the LORD.
—PSALM 111:3–4

I visited many ancient ruins while living in the Middle East
years ago. I saw firsthand the architectural designs that
have withstood centuries of change. The psalmist knew
that God's "wise design endures forever." This applies not
only to the physical universe but also to the human soul.
We were built to last. And we should live each day as if our
actions will influence the world generations from now.

2 Corinthians 11:1–11
Psalm 111
Matthew 6:7–15

Friday

JUNE 17

But store up treasures in heaven, where neither moth nor decay destroy, nor thieves break in and steal. For where your treasure is, there also will your heart be.

—MATTHEW 6:20–21

Even though Kurt was in good health, he spent several weeks preparing to die. He went through his possessions, reconnected with people, and put his affairs in order. When he was finished, he looked at life differently. His priorities had changed. His "treasure" was no longer a better title at work or a car with more options. Now he valued peace, time with those he loved, and activities that made the world a better place.

2 Corinthians 11:18, 21–30
Psalm 34
Matthew 6:19–23

No one can serve two masters. He will either hate one and love the other, or be devoted to one and despise the other. You cannot serve God and mammon.

—MATTHEW 6:24

Early in her career, Erin understood that the company she worked for would take every hour of her day and every ounce of her energy if she allowed it to. The corporate culture did not respect her whole life, which included a family and involvement in a church community. So Erin drew boundaries and watched others get promoted at work. She was at peace, however, knowing that her family and community life would fulfill her long after her work life had ended.

2 Corinthians 12:1–10
Psalm 34
Matthew 6:24–34

JUNE 19

• FATHER'S DAY •

O LORD of hosts, you who test the just,
who probe mind and heart,
Let me witness the vengeance you take on them,
for to you I have entrusted my cause.

—JEREMIAH 20:12

It's difficult for a Christian to comprehend Scriptures that speak positively of vengeance. Jesus taught us not to take vengeance. Yet these verses were written at a time when there was little understanding of grace, forgiveness, or rehabilitation; people were either allies or enemies. What is significant about Jeremiah's attitude is that he understood God's wisdom about people. He trusted God to sift the truth out from the lies, and he knew that his own cause was best left in God's hands.

Jeremiah 20:10–13
Psalm 69
Romans 5:12–15
Matthew 10:26–33

The LORD said to Abram: "Go forth from the land of your kinsfolk and from your father's house to a land that I will show you."
—GENESIS 12:1

Have you ever been asked to leave behind everything that is familiar in order to begin a new phase in your life? Abraham left the land of his people and thus put himself outside the tribal structure that had always provided identity, resources, and protection. He did it because God called him. To what life is God calling you?

Genesis 12:1–9
Psalm 33
Matthew 7:1–5

Enter through the narrow gate; for the gate is wide and the road broad that leads to destruction, and those who enter through it are many. How narrow the gate and constricted the road that leads to life. And those who find it are few.

—MATTHEW 7:13–14

In this well-known passage, Jesus warns us about the path of least resistance. True life requires us to pay attention, make sacrifices, and act wisely. And, as so many great reformers have proven, living such a life often means going against common practice or the accepted point of view. Ask yourself today, "Am I doing this because it's the right thing to do or because it takes the least amount of effort?"

Genesis 13:2, 5–18
Psalm 15
Matthew 7:6, 12–14

Beware of false prophets, who come to you in sheep's clothing, but underneath are ravenous wolves. By their fruits you will know them. Do people pick grapes from thornbushes, or figs from thistles?

—MATTHEW 7:15–16

Don heard so many horror stories about a certain religious organization that he and his business partner began to investigate. They spent years talking to individuals, families, and entire congregations that had been torn apart by one man's "ministry." The man had charisma and glossy programming, and he'd achieved popularity throughout the country. But his "fruit" revealed the true story.

Genesis 15:1–12, 17–18
Psalm 105
Matthew 7:15–20

Many times did he rescue them,
but they kept rebelling and scheming
and were brought low by their own guilt.
Still God had regard for their affliction
when he heard their wailing.

—PSALM 106:43–44

How many times have I schemed to get my own way or rebelled against the God I know to be true? Why do you even attend to me, God, when I mess up and come running to you for assistance? Help me look at the unhealthy patterns in my life and follow your guidance more willingly.

Genesis 16:1–12, 15–16 or 16:6–12, 15–16
Psalm 106
Matthew 7:21–29

Friday
JUNE 24

*It was revealed to [the prophets] that they were serving not themselves
but you with regard to the things that have now been announced to you
by those who preached the good news to you [through] the holy Spirit
sent from heaven, things into which angels longed to look.*

—1 PETER 1:12

True prophets of God know that their lives and words go
far beyond their particular time and place. Prophets are in
service to the rest of us. They proclaim promises and hope
for glimpses of their fulfillment, knowing that others will
experience what they proclaim. Unlike self-declared
prophets who collect followers and build their own
empires, God's prophets give all they are to God and, in
turn, to us.

Vigil:	Day:
Jeremiah 1:4–10	Isaiah 49:1–6
Psalm 71	Psalm 139
1 Peter 1:8–12	Acts 13:22–26
Luke 1:5–17	Luke 1:57–66, 80

[T]he LORD said to Abraham: "Why did Sarah laugh and say, 'Shall I really bear a child, old as I am?' Is anything too marvelous for the LORD to do? At the appointed time, about this time next year, I will return to you, and Sarah will have a son."

—GENESIS 18:13–14

Lord, you mildly rebuked Sarah for doubting what you could do. When have I doubted you? When have I laughed at the prospect of what you had in store for me?

Genesis 18:1–15
Luke 1:46–50, 53–55
Matthew 8:5–17

If, then, we have died with Christ, we believe that we shall also live with him. . . . Consequently, you too must think of yourselves as [being] dead to sin and living for God in Christ Jesus.

—ROMANS 6:8, 11

How much do you identify with Christ? When you suffer, do you consider it part of Christ's suffering? When you look to the future, do you see yourself sharing in Christ's glory and freedom? Try to go through today imagining that Christ is beside you at every moment, experiencing what you are experiencing.

2 Kings 4:8–11, 14–16
Psalm 89
Romans 6:3–4, 8–11
Matthew 10:37–42

The LORD replied, "If I find fifty innocent people in the city of Sodom, I will spare the whole place for their sake." . . . But [Abraham] still persisted, "Please, let not my Lord grow angry if I speak up this last time. What if there are at least ten there?" "For the sake of those ten," he replied, "I will not destroy it."

—GENESIS 18:26, 32

Here is Abraham, bargaining with almighty God. And God bargains with Abraham, seemingly unperturbed by the man's assertiveness. This story demonstrates God's patience toward our prayers. Perhaps we, too, should approach God with more confidence and honesty.

Genesis 18:16–33
Psalm 103
Matthew 8:18–22

As dawn was breaking, the angels urged Lot on, saying, "On your way! Take with you your wife and your two daughters who are here, or you will be swept away in the punishment of the city." When he hesitated, the men, by the LORD's mercy, seized his hand and the hands of his wife and his two daughters and led them to safety outside the city.

—GENESIS 19:15–16

I have always been touched by the image of the angels taking these people by the hand and leading them to safety when they were too stymied to move by themselves. I wonder how many times God has grabbed my hand when I was paralyzed by fear or indecision. How many times have I made it to safety because of God's care? How many people has God placed in my life for the express purpose of helping me take action?

Genesis 19:15–29
Psalm 26
Matthew 8:23–27

When they had finished breakfast, Jesus said to Simon Peter, "Simon, son of John, do you love me more than these?" He said to him, "Yes, Lord, you know that I love you." He said to him, "Feed my lambs."

—JOHN 21:15

Thanks to Peter, Paul, and men and women after them who took it upon themselves to feed Jesus' lambs, the church has thrived for two millennia. May we give special thanks for them today, and may we recognize those among us now who, as our shepherds, care for us as God's own.

<table>
<tr><td>Vigil:</td><td>Day:</td></tr>
<tr><td>Acts 3:1–10</td><td>Acts 12:1–11</td></tr>
<tr><td>Psalm 19</td><td>Psalm 34</td></tr>
<tr><td>Galatians 1:11–20</td><td>2 Timothy 4:6–8, 17–18</td></tr>
<tr><td>John 21:15–19</td><td>Matthew 16:13–19</td></tr>
</table>

Thursday

JUNE 30

• THE FIRST HOLY MARTYRS OF THE HOLY ROMAN CHURCH •

As the two walked on together, Isaac spoke to his father Abraham:
"Father!" he said. . . . "Here are the fire and the wood, but where is the
sheep for the holocaust?" "Son," Abraham answered, "God himself will
provide the sheep for the holocaust." Then the two continued going
forward.

—GENESIS 22:7–8

Just as Abraham was willing to sacrifice his son, so the first
martyrs of the church in Rome willingly gave their lives to
God. God spared Isaac's life, but we are not always spared.

Are we willing to "continue going forward" anyway?

Genesis 22:1–19
Psalm 115
Matthew 9:1–8

Friday

JULY 1

• BLESSED JUNÍPERO SERRA, PRIEST •

*As Jesus passed on from there, he saw a man named Matthew sitting
at the customs post. He said to him, "Follow me." And he got up and
followed him.*

—MATTHEW 9:9

Some decisions require much deliberation. But others we can
make instantaneously, as if we have been preparing for them
all our life. God's hand is in those decisions—although we
are unaware of it, the Lord readies us for decisions we will
make days, months, and even years from now.

Genesis 23:1–4, 19; 24:1–8, 62–67
Psalm 106
Matthew 9:9–13

People do not put new wine into old wineskins. Otherwise the skins burst, the wine spills out, and the skins are ruined. Rather, they pour new wine into fresh wineskins, and both are preserved.

—MATTHEW 9:17

I'd been struggling to learn contemplative prayer, and then I realized I hadn't learned the larger lesson about creating quiet in every aspect of my life. I can take in all sorts of new information about how to live, how to pray, and how to relate to others. But unless I adjust my lifestyle to contain that information, it will be wasted on me.

Genesis 27:1–5, 15–29
Psalm 135
Matthew 9:14–17

Come to me, all you who labor and are burdened, and I will give you rest. Take my yoke upon you and learn from me, for I am meek and humble of heart; and you will find rest for yourselves.

—MATTHEW 11:28–29

So much of the weight we carry is merely our own resistance to carrying anything at all. We can rest in Jesus because he understands how to carry burdens. A "meek and humble" heart is one that surrenders to God.

Zechariah 9:9–10
Psalm 145
Romans 8:9, 11–13
Matthew 11:25–30

Monday

JULY 4

• SAINT ELIZABETH OF PORTUGAL • INDEPENDENCE DAY •

When Jacob awoke from his sleep, he exclaimed, "Truly, the LORD is
in this spot, although I did not know it!"
—GENESIS 28:16

When they tore down the abandoned building, they found
a photo album, long forgotten, containing pictures of
children with labels identifying them as foster kids who
had lived in that home. Some pictures were accompanied
by short notes reporting happy endings: this child had
married, another had joined the military. No one had lived
in these rooms for years, but it was evident that miracles
had once happened here.

Genesis 28:10–22
Psalm 91
Matthew 9:18–26

────────────

Then he said to his disciples, "The harvest is abundant but the laborers are few; so ask the master of the harvest to send out laborers for his harvest."

—MATTHEW 9:37–38

Most people are readier to respond to God than they appear. It is the rare person who has little or no interest in the spiritual life. We don't have to be forceful to be laborers of the harvest. Sometimes just a simple question or comment can cause a person to open up her heart.

Genesis 32:23–33
Psalm 17
Matthew 9:32–38

Then he summoned his twelve disciples and gave them authority over unclean spirits to drive them out and to cure every disease and every illness.

—MATTHEW 10:1

Jesus, we forget that you still give us power today to do your work. Give us hearts to understand your work within us. Give us the courage to step up and expect miracles.

Genesis 41:55–57; 42:5–7, 17–24
Psalm 33
Matthew 10:1–7

Thursday

JULY 7

Cure the sick, raise the dead, cleanse lepers, drive out demons. Without cost you have received; without cost you are to give.

—MATTHEW 10:8

Gratefulness nearly always leads to service. When we realize what we have received through no merit of our own, our thoughts toward others grow more generous.

Genesis 44:18–21, 23–29; 45:1–5
Psalm 105
Matthew 10:7–15

⇒ 224 ⇐

Friday

JULY 8

The mouths of the just utter wisdom;
their tongues speak what is right.
God's teaching is in their hearts;
their steps do not falter.
—PSALM 37:30–31

Lord, the life I want is one that integrates your teaching
into all my words and steps.

Genesis 46:1–7, 28–30
Psalm 37
Matthew 10:16–23

• SAINT AUGUSTINE ZHAO RONG, PRIEST AND MARTYR, AND HIS
COMPANIONS, MARTYRS •

*Even though you meant harm to me, God meant it for good, to achieve
his present end, the survival of many people.*

—GENESIS 50:20

God can take even the harmful intentions and actions of
others and bring them to a beneficial end. No experience is
wasted.

Genesis 49:29–32; 50:15–26
Psalm 105
Matthew 10:24–33

Sunday

JULY 10

The seed sown on rocky ground is the one who hears the word and receives it at once with joy. But he has no root and lasts only for a time. When some tribulation or persecution comes because of the word, he immediately falls away.

—MATTHEW 13:20–21

Enthusiasm does not always indicate strong faith. Unfortunately, we sometimes mistake enthusiasm in new converts for maturity and give them more responsibility than they can bear—which makes it even likelier that they will burn out and fall away.

Isaiah 55:10–11
Psalm 65
Romans 8:18–23
Matthew 13:1–23 or 13:1–9

Whoever receives you receives me, and whoever receives me receives the one who sent me.

—MATTHEW 10:40

In some mysterious way I carry Christ within me, and when people encounter me they make contact with Christ. This is hard to understand, but it's encouraging to think of myself as a connection between others and the God who seeks them.

Exodus 1:8–14, 22
Psalm 124
Matthew 10:34–11:1

I have become an outcast to my kin,
a stranger to my mother's children.
Because zeal for your house consumes me,
I am scorned by those who scorn you.

—PSALM 69:9–10

Both of the men were converts to Christianity in a country that forbade conversion upon threat of death. They met in the home of foreigners, a safe place for them to talk about their newfound faith. They both wept from relief; they had lived months without any fellowship at all, without a single person with whom to share their spiritual life.

Exodus 2:1–15
Psalm 69
Matthew 11:20–24

Wednesday

JULY 13

• SAINT HENRY •

"I am the God of your father," he continued, "the God of Abraham, the God of Isaac, the God of Jacob."

—EXODUS 3:6

When faith in God has existed in former generations of our family, this spiritual heritage strengthens us. When we meet God personally, we can be encouraged to know that this is the same God who has been in relationship with our parents, grandparents, great-grandparents, and so on. Spiritual pathways have already been marked out within our family, and we can draw from the experience of those who have preceded us.

Exodus 3:1–6, 9–12
Psalm 103
Matthew 11:25–27

∋ 230 ∈

When they were few in number,
a handful, and strangers there,
Wandering from nation to nation,
from one kingdom to another,
He let no one oppress them;
for their sake he rebuked kings.
—PSALM 105:12–14

When the Lord is with us, we will succeed in our journey.
When the Lord walks beside us, we need no other
companions.

Exodus 3:13–20
Psalm 105
Matthew 11:28–30

⇒ 231 ⇐

I love the LORD, who listened
to my voice in supplication,
Who turned an ear to me
on the day I called.
—PSALM 116:1–2

The person we trust most is the one we can count on when we're in trouble. The psalmist remembered that God was there when trouble came. If we remembered more often those times when God heard our cries for help, wouldn't our trust be steadier?

Exodus 11:10–12:14
Psalm 116
Matthew 12:1–8

Saturday

JULY 16

• OUR LADY OF MOUNT CARMEL •

*At the end of four hundred and thirty years, all the hosts of the LORD
left the land of Egypt on this very date. This was a night of vigil for
the LORD, as he led them out of the land of Egypt; so on this same
night all the Israelites must keep a vigil for the LORD throughout their
generations.*

—EXODUS 12:41–42

Anisa's family still celebrates the anniversary of the day her
great-great-grandmother arrived at Ellis Island. Enrique's
family commemorates the day that his brother, a political
prisoner, was released from prison. What dates and
anniversaries are sacred in your family? What journeys and
arrivals define you even now?

Exodus 12:37–42
Psalm 136
Matthew 12:14–21

⇒ 233 ⇐

[T]he Spirit too comes to the aid of our weakness; for we do not know how to pray as we ought, but the Spirit itself intercedes with inexpressible groanings.

—ROMANS 8:26

Holy Spirit, you join my spirit when I pray, making my thoughts holy and complete. You sift through my desires and fears and turn them into meaningful communication. You take my sighs and tears and translate them to heaven. Thank you for being my companion.

Wisdom 12:13, 16–19
Psalm 86
Romans 8:26–27
Matthew 13:24–43 or 13:24–30

Monday

JULY 18

• SAINT CAMILLUS DE LELLIS, PRIEST •

I will sing to the LORD, for he is gloriously triumphant;
horse and chariot he has cast into the sea.

—EXODUS 15:1

The Israelites sang this after God parted the Red Sea to
allow them to flee the Egyptians. Forever they would carry
with them the image of horses and chariots being thrown
into the sea. What image would represent God's
deliverance in *your* life?

Exodus 14:5–18
Exodus 15:1–6
Matthew 12:38–42

⇒ 235 ⇐

At a breath of your anger the waters piled up,
the flowing waters stood like a mound,
the flood waters congealed in the midst of the sea.
—EXODUS 15:8

In the oral tradition of the Hebrews, poetry played an important role in helping the people remember their history with God. What form of art has enhanced your life of faith? Can you think of some new form to pursue for that purpose?

Exodus 14:21–15:1
Exodus 15:8–10, 12, 17
Matthew 12:46–50

I will open my mouth in story,
drawing lessons from of old.
We have heard them, we know them;
our ancestors have recited them to us.

—PSALM 78:2–3

We remember stories long after we've forgotten facts and figures. The heroes in our favorite books from childhood continue to shape our character even when we have children of our own. And our family stories keep memory alive, from one generation to the next. Spend some time today recalling a story or telling a story to someone else.

Exodus 16:1–5, 9–15
Psalm 78
Matthew 13:1–9

Thursday

JULY 21

Blessed are you who look into the depths
from your throne upon the cherubim,
praiseworthy and exalted above all forever.
—DANIEL 3:55

When I realize how broad your vision is, holy God, I remember how small I am. I am just another human being on a planet of many human beings, and this planet is but a speck in the universe. Yet you look "into the depths" not only of the universe but also of my single heart. Your attentiveness to my life makes me honorable, even significant, in this vast world.

Exodus 19:1–2, 9–11, 16–20
Daniel 3:52–56
Matthew 13:10–17

Friday

JULY 22

• SAINT MARY MAGDALENE •

On the first day of the week, Mary of Magdala came to the tomb early in the morning, while it was still dark, and saw the stone removed from the tomb.

—JOHN 20:1

Jesus had cast seven demons from Mary Magdalene. We can imagine the grief and longing that compelled her through the darkness to his grave. She eventually saw the risen Jesus. But first she had to face that gaping tomb. Each of us comes to such a moment, when we have lost the person or thing in which we've placed our hope. We can only trust that this bleak emptiness is part of God's plan for us.

Exodus 20:1–17
Psalm 63
John 20:1–2, 11–18

When the crop grew and bore fruit, the weeds appeared as well. The slaves of the householder came to him and said, "Master, did you not sow good seed in your field? Where have the weeds come from?"

—MATTHEW 13:26–27

Sometimes I look at my work, remember my good intentions and hours of labor, and ask, "Where did these weeds come from?" Problems sprout no matter what I do. I take comfort in this parable, in which the "master" is Jesus. Weeds pop up in his field, too, but in the parable he explains that he will wait for the crop to ripen and then sort the good from the bad. I can learn to do the same.

Exodus 24:3–8
Psalm 50
Matthew 13:24–30

In Gibeon the LORD appeared to Solomon in a dream at night. God said, "Ask something of me and I will give it to you." . . . "Give your servant . . . an understanding heart to judge your people and to distinguish right from wrong. For who is able to govern this vast people of yours?"

—1 KINGS 3:5, 9

Solomon could have asked for riches or victory in battle, but he asked for wisdom instead. Help us, Lord, to always seek the best things.

1 Kings 3:5, 7–12
Psalm 119
Romans 8:28–30
Matthew 13:44–52 or 13:44–46

[T]he Son of Man did not come to be served but to serve and to give his life as a ransom for many.

—MATTHEW 20:28

Jesus, you changed the definition of leadership. You taught us, first of all, how to be servants, how to think of others before ourselves. Two thousand years have passed, and most of the world still tries to lead by domination. Help us cultivate your spirit of service wherever we go.

2 Corinthians 4:7–15
Psalm 126
Matthew 20:20–28

The LORD used to speak to Moses face to face, as one man speaks to another.

—EXODUS 33:11

Just when I've decided that God is distant and not personally involved with me, I come upon a passage such as this. Somehow God stands apart from humanity and yet deals with people intimately. I don't understand how this is so, but knowing that God speaks to me face-to-face makes it easier to pray.

Exodus 33:7–11; 34:5–9, 28
Psalm 132
Matthew 13:36–43

[T]he kingdom of heaven is like a merchant searching for fine pearls.
When he finds a pearl of great price, he goes and sells all that he has
and buys it.

—MATTHEW 13:45–46

She had to have the painting. It told stories in vivid colors,
and she could feel her very soul respond. It cost an entire
paycheck, but she was willing to pass up many other
expenses just to own that single piece of art. She hoped
that she would always be able to see what was most
valuable and to let go of lesser treasures.

Exodus 34:29–35
Psalm 99
Matthew 13:44–46

Thursday

JULY 28

Happy are those who find refuge in you,
whose hearts are set on pilgrim roads.
As they pass through the Baca valley,
they find spring water to drink.
Also from pools the Lord provides water
for those who lose their way.

—PSALM 84:6–7

Finding refuge is crucial for those of us traveling "pilgrim roads," whether those roads are part of literal or spiritual journeys. The psalmist describes the Lord's provision of refuge and help, even to those who have lost their way. It's encouraging to know that when our hearts are set on the journey, God's love provides, whether we are on the right track or wandering in confusion.

Exodus 40:16–21, 34–38
Psalm 84
Matthew 13:47–53

Friday

JULY 29

Martha said to Jesus, "Lord, if you had been here, my brother would not have died. [But] even now I know that whatever you ask of God, God will give you."

—JOHN 11:21–22

Do you find yourself identifying with Martha? Does your pragmatism sometimes interfere with your believing wholeheartedly in God's care for you? If so, you can take heart in the fact that Martha grew in faith by simply being in Jesus' presence. By spending time with him, she was able to see beyond the practical and experience astounding hope.

Leviticus 23:1, 4–11, 15–16, 27, 34–37
Psalm 81
John 11:19–27 or Luke 10:38–42

This fiftieth year you shall make sacred by proclaiming liberty in the land for all its inhabitants. It shall be a jubilee for you, when every one of you shall return to his own property, every one to his own family estate.

—LEVITICUS 25:10

The Jubilee every fifty years prevented ancient Hebrew families from losing their inheritances permanently. Land that had been sold to other families could be bought back at a fair price. With this law, the Lord confirmed the importance of family place. In honor of God's justice, give thanks today for your home and pray for families all over the world who have been displaced, their homes stolen or destroyed.

Leviticus 25:1, 8–17
Psalm 67
Matthew 14:1–12

I am convinced that neither death, nor life, nor angels, nor principalities,
nor present things, nor future things, nor powers, nor height, nor depth,
nor any other creature will be able to separate us from the love of God
in Christ Jesus our Lord.

—ROMANS 8:38–39

No matter what trial or heartbreak or obstacle you face, it
cannot keep God from loving you. Write Romans 8:38–39
on a slip of paper and place it where you will see it often.

Isaiah 55:1–3
Psalm 145
Romans 8:35, 37–39
Matthew 14:13–21

I cannot carry all this people by myself, for they are too heavy for me.
If this is the way you will deal with me, then please do me the favor of
killing me at once, so that I need no longer face this distress.

—NUMBERS 11:14–15

What a prayer! Moses was fed up with his job and with the
people God had put in his charge. Yet Moses did reach the
end of his journey, and eventually Joshua was given the
task of leading the Hebrews into the Promised Land. We
can be comforted by Moses' honesty. Are we willing to talk
to God so bluntly?

Numbers 11:4–15
Psalm 81
Matthew 14:22–36

Tuesday

AUGUST 2

• SAINT EUSEBIUS OF VERCELLI, BISHOP •
• SAINT PETER JULIAN EYMARD, PRIEST •

*For you do not desire sacrifice;
a burnt offering you would not accept.
My sacrifice, God, is a broken spirit;
God, do not spurn a broken, humbled heart.*

—PSALM 51:18–19

Even when the Jewish sacrificial system was in force, this
writer understood that what truly got God's attention was a
humble and open spirit; the sacrifice itself was not enough.
How do you try to get God's attention? By doing all the
"right" things? By forming relationships with the "right"
people? By punishing yourself for not being perfect? Offer
God your heart instead.

Numbers 12:1–13
Psalm 51
Matthew 14:22–36 or 15:1–2, 10–14

"We went into the land to which you sent us. It does indeed flow with milk and honey. . . . However, the people who are living in the land are fierce, and the towns are fortified and very strong." . . . So they spread discouraging reports among the Israelites.

—NUMBERS 13:27–28, 32

Because ten of the twelve scouts Moses sent to Canaan reported only on the fierce people there and expressed no confidence in God's help, the Israelites decided not to settle in the land and were forced to travel another forty years in the wilderness. It really does matter how we present the facts. When we are put in positions of authority, our first task is to offer hope and guidance to those in our charge.

Numbers 13:1–2, 25–14:1, 26–29, 34–35
Psalm 106
Matthew 15:21–28

Jesus said to him in reply, "Blessed are you, Simon son of Jonah. For flesh and blood has not revealed this to you, but my heavenly Father. . . . I will give you the keys to the kingdom of heaven. Whatever you bind on earth shall be bound in heaven; and whatever you loose on earth shall be loosed in heaven."

—MATTHEW 16:17, 19

John Vianney was not an outstanding student of the priesthood, and he was dispatched to an unremarkable parish. But he had the gift of spiritual discernment, and because of this he was a great confessor. People came from all around to be counseled by him. God gave St. John Vianney the keys to others' hearts, possibly the greatest gift of all.

Numbers 20:1–13
Psalm 95
Matthew 16:13–23

Then Jesus said to his disciples, "Whoever wishes to come after me must deny himself, take up his cross, and follow me."
—MATTHEW 16:24

A preacher once said, "You can choose the road you take, but you cannot choose where that road takes you." This is what Jesus was saying, too. By taking up our cross and following him, we identify with him completely. We take on the values of God's kingdom, and we simply follow, not knowing where the journey will take us.

Deuteronomy 4:32–40
Psalm 77
Matthew 16:24–28

Saturday

AUGUST 6

• THE TRANSFIGURATION OF THE LORD •

And he was transfigured before them; his face shone like the sun and his clothes became white as light. And behold, Moses and Elijah appeared to them, conversing with him.

—MATTHEW 17:2–3

This Christian faith is full of mystery that involves past, present, and future. Who knows what souls walk with us without our even knowing it? If we considered the wonders of the spiritual realm more often, how would it affect our outlook?

Daniel 7:9–10, 13–14
Psalm 97
2 Peter 1:16–19
Matthew 17:1–9

AUGUST 7

There he came to a cave, where he took shelter. But the word of the LORD came to him, "Why are you here, Elijah?"

—1 KINGS 19:9

We can run, but we can't hide! When stressful circumstances have us running here and there, God's first question is usually, "Why are you here?" And when we answer that question, already we understand more about ourselves. The Holy Spirit will continue to teach us self-reflection.

1 Kings 19:9, 11–13
Psalm 85
Romans 9:1–5
Matthew 14:22–33

[T]he LORD, your God, is the God of gods, the LORD of lords, the great God, mighty and awesome, who has no favorites, accepts no bribes; who executes justice for the orphan and the widow, and befriends the alien, feeding and clothing him.

—DEUTERONOMY 10:17–18

The kids in the group home complained plenty about the director's strict rules. They acted as if they didn't like him at all. But they trusted him completely and took their problems to his office, because even if he wasn't their buddy, the man was fair. He required that they be fair, too. For several of the kids there, it was the first time they had ever felt safe.

Deuteronomy 10:12–22
Psalm 147
Matthew 17:22–27

Tuesday

AUGUST 9

• SAINT TERESA BENEDICTA OF THE CROSS (EDITH STEIN),
VIRGIN AND MARTYR •

*It is the LORD who marches before you; he will be with you and will
never fail you or forsake you. So do not fear or be dismayed.*
—DEUTERONOMY 31:8

A Jewish philosopher who converted to Catholicism,
St. Teresa Benedicta—also known as Edith Stein—died in
the gas chambers of Auschwitz in 1942. Today, her feast
day, we can reflect on these words of Moses to Joshua. The
Lord accompanies his sons and daughters whatever their
destiny, whether it is to enter the literal Promised Land or
to die for his sake and enter paradise.

Deuteronomy 31:1–8
Deuteronomy 32:3–4, 7–9, 12
Matthew 18:1–5, 10, 12–14

Amen, amen, I say to you, unless a grain of wheat falls to the ground and dies, it remains just a grain of wheat; but if it dies, it produces much fruit.

—JOHN 12:24

According to the poet Prudentius, idolatry in Rome declined significantly after St. Lawrence was martyred. But we don't have to die physically in order to bear fruit. Sometimes our goals, ideas, and preferences must die. Or we have to put to death our own power and allow God's power to grow within us. Whatever the case, God brings from our sacrifice new life.

2 Corinthians 9:6–10
Psalm 112
John 12:24–26

AUGUST 11

• SAINT CLARE, VIRGIN •

The people struck their tents to cross the Jordan, with the priests carrying the ark of the covenant ahead of them. No sooner had these priestly bearers of the ark waded into the waters at the edge of the Jordan . . . than the waters flowing from upstream halted, backing up in a solid mass for a very great distance indeed.

—JOSHUA 3:14–16

When the priests bearing God's ark stepped into the river, it stopped its course. Did that really happen? What about other miracles in the Bible? Is the factual credibility the real point? Perhaps the critical issue is what happens in the human imagination when the story is told. The mind is able to reshape its expectations, and the heart can learn to dwell with mystery.

Joshua 3:7–11, 13–17
Psalm 114
Matthew 18:21–19:1

Friday

AUGUST 12

I gave you a land which you had not tilled and cities which you had not built, to dwell in; you have eaten of vineyards and olive groves which you did not plant.

—JOSHUA 24:13

Are you comfortable receiving gifts? Or must you somehow deserve the good things in your life? Can you admit that you owe your abilities—and therefore your successes—in part to the generosity of others? If nothing else, you have to give credit to being born to a certain family in a certain place and having had access to particular opportunities. Each of us, to some degree, harvests what others plant.

Joshua 24:1–13
Psalm 136
Matthew 19:3–12

*Then [Joshua] took a large stone and set it up there under the oak that
was in the sanctuary of the LORD. And Joshua said to all the people,
"This stone shall be our witness, for it has heard all the words which
the LORD spoke to us."*

—JOSHUA 24:26–27

While preparing her parents' home for auction, Rachel
spent a day lingering in the house and garden. She was
drawn to the bench near the rose bushes; this was where
her mother had prayed in the evenings, sometimes holding
Rachel as she asked God's blessings on their home. Rachel
decided to move the bench to her own backyard. It was a
simple slab of stone, but in this family's life it had become
a holy place.

Joshua 24:14–29
Psalm 16
Matthew 19:13–15

———

AUGUST 14

*[M]y house shall be called
a house of prayer for all peoples.*
—ISAIAH 56:7

After the disaster, no one asked whose building it was. No
one noticed if it was decorated with a cross, the Star of
David, or a crescent moon. People filled the sanctuary
respectfully, stood close, held hands, prayed for the dead
and missing, organized relief efforts. They were extremely
kind to one another. Thus their experience of worship
expanded. And the building became a house of prayer in a
whole new way.

Isaiah 56:1, 6–7
Psalm 67
Romans 11:13–15, 29–32
Matthew 15:21–28

A great sign appeared in the sky, a woman clothed with the sun. . . . She was with child and wailed aloud in pain as she labored to give birth. . . . She gave birth to a son, a male child, destined to rule all the nations with an iron rod. Her child was caught up to God and his throne.

—REVELATION 12:1–2, 5

The world will always need a mother, a woman who represents divinity at its most intimate and nurturing. Mary the Jewish girl became the mother of Jesus and eventually became a saint. She has reappeared in visions and legends ever since. Thus she has become a mother to all of us who struggle to respond to God's beckoning.

Vigil:	**Day:**
1 Chronicles 15:3–4, 15–16; 16:1–2	Revelation 11:19; 12:1–6, 10
Psalm 132	Psalm 45
1 Corinthians 15:54–57	1 Corinthians 15:20–27
Luke 11:27–28	Luke 1:39–56

The LORD turned to him and said, "Go with the strength you have and save Israel from the power of Midian. It is I who send you."

—JUDGES 6:14

Go with the strength you have. Are we willing to step up and do great things using the resources we already have, or do we wait until we are stronger, richer, more educated, more influential? If God sends us, will God not also make it possible for us to succeed?

Judges 6:11–24
Psalm 85
Matthew 19:23–30

AUGUST 17

"These last ones worked only one hour, and you have made them equal to us, who bore the day's burden and the heat." He said to one of them in reply. . . . "[A]m I not free to do as I wish with my own money? Are you envious because I am generous?" Thus, the last will be first, and the first will be last.

—MATTHEW 20:12–16

I'm always speaking up for justice and equality. But do I feel as strongly about God's *generosity*? Do I rejoice when undeserving people get lucky? Am I happy when horrible people turn to faith at their last breath and are received gladly into Jesus' embrace? God's mercy goes far beyond my sensibilities. To understand it fully, I must pray for a change of heart.

Judges 9:6–15
Psalm 21
Matthew 20:1–16

AUGUST 18

• SAINT JANE FRANCES DE CHANTAL, RELIGIOUS •

I waited, waited for the LORD;
who bent down and heard my cry,
Drew me out of the pit of destruction,
out of the mud of the swamp,
Set my feet upon rock,
steadied my steps,
And put a new song in my mouth,
a hymn to our God.
—PSALM 40:2–4

You were up to your knees (or your neck) in trouble. But suddenly the situation shifted and your mind cleared, and you knew what to do. In a short time, your whole life changed. That transformation was the work of God, and the relief that flooded you is raw material for true praise.

Judges 11:29–39
Psalm 40
Matthew 22:1–14

Ruth said, "Do not ask me to abandon or forsake you! for wherever you go I will go, wherever you lodge I will lodge, your people shall be my people, and your God my God."

—RUTH 1:16

Ruth's decision to leave behind the life she knew and follow her mother-in-law ultimately resulted in her becoming the great-grandmother of King David. But she had no way of foreseeing this. Perhaps Ruth was led to her decision by the faith that shaped her mother-in-law, or perhaps she saw glimmers of the true God even as both she and Naomi grieved the deaths of their husbands. Whatever the reason, Ruth set upon a journey, and God prepared her path.

Ruth 1:1, 3–6, 14–16, 22
Psalm 146
Matthew 22:34–40

Then Jesus spoke to the crowds and to his disciples, saying, "The scribes and the Pharisees have taken their seat on the chair of Moses. Therefore, do and observe all things whatsoever they tell you, but do not follow their example. For they preach but they do not practice."

—MATTHEW 23:1–3

The director of the discipleship ministry was not only a dynamic Bible teacher but also a charismatic leader. He trained many young Christians to be good teachers as well. We can only hope they did not follow his example, however. After several years, his wife divorced him; in his zeal for the work, he had badly neglected their relationship, so wounding her emotionally that she could not carry on.

Ruth 2:1–3, 8–11; 4:13–17
Psalm 128
Matthew 23:1–12

AUGUST 21

The LORD is with me to the end.
LORD, your love endures forever.
Never forsake the work of your hands!
—PSALM 138:8

During the 1980s, the phrase "God is not finished with me yet" became popular in some circles. What a healthy way to look at the life of faith. God stays with you, always loves you, and never stops working on your life. May you be more patient with yourself as you trust this lifelong process.

Isaiah 22:19–23
Psalm 138
Romans 11:33–36
Matthew 16:13–20

For from you the word of the Lord has sounded forth not only in Macedonia and [in] Achaia, but in every place your faith in God has gone forth, so that we have no need to say anything.

—1 THESSALONIANS 1:8

Christians from the free world have been amazed to find the church quite alive in places where it was presumed dead—the former Soviet Union or Communist China, for example. Wherever believers live in faith, God's grace is allowed to continue its work, and the word spreads, in good times and bad.

1 Thessalonians 1:1–5, 8–10
Psalm 149
Matthew 23:13–22

Tuesday

AUGUST 23

• SAINT ROSE OF LIMA, VIRGIN •

My travels and my rest you mark;
with all my ways you are familiar.
Even before a word is on my tongue,
LORD, you know it all.
Behind and before you encircle me
and rest your hand upon me.
—PSALM 139:3–5

What a comfort it is, Lord, that you know me so well,
better than I know myself. I don't understand how you
could love me so much while seeing my sins and failures.
But you surround me completely. Like a mother with a small
child, you are constantly close at hand, attending to me.

1 Thessalonians 2:1–8
Psalm 139
Matthew 23:23–26

Jesus saw Nathanael coming toward him and said of him, "Here is a
true Israelite. There is no duplicity in him." Nathanael said to him,
"How do you know me?" Jesus answered and said to him, "Before
Philip called you, I saw you under the fig tree."

—JOHN 1:47–48

Jesus is watching us before we even desire to know him or
follow him. When we turn to faith, we think we are
beginning a new life. But our life of faith has been
progressing, under his observance, for a long time,
although we have been unaware of it. In this way,
embracing faith is like becoming conscious of our souls for
the first time.

Revelation 21:9–14
Psalm 145
John 1:45–51

Thursday

AUGUST 25

• SAINT JOSEPH CALASANZ, PRIEST • SAINT LOUIS OF FRANCE •

Night and day we pray beyond measure to see you in person and to remedy the deficiencies of your faith. Now may God himself, our Father, and our Lord Jesus direct our way to you, and may the Lord make you increase and abound in love for one another and for all, just as we have for you.

—1 THESSALONIANS 3:10–12

May we be this concerned about the "soul life" of the people we love. Paul was a teacher who strove to communicate the tenets of faith in Jesus. Whether or not we, too, are teachers or spiritual counselors, we can be passionate about encouraging others in their faith.

1 Thessalonians 3:7–13
Psalm 90
Matthew 24:42–51

Light dawns for the just;
gladness, for the honest of heart.
Rejoice in the LORD, you just,
and praise his holy name.
—PSALM 97:11–12

Against all odds, attorney Morris Dees went after the Ku
Klux Klan for the murder of a young black man. In a
moving statement, the mother of the boy expressed her
forgiveness for the killers when she spoke before the court.
The result of the trial? The Klan lost its headquarters
building, which went to the boy's mother.

1 Thessalonians 4:1–8
Psalm 97
Matthew 25:1–13

Well done, my good and faithful servant. Since you were faithful in small matters, I will give you great responsibilities. Come, share your master's joy.

—MATTHEW 25:23

He was just a paperboy who worked a route in a Chicago suburb. But he was a conscientious paperboy, and one of his customers noticed. The customer had his own optics shop and ground lenses for various companies, including NASA. He apprenticed the paperboy, and within just a few years, the paperboy had a career in optics. He who is faithful in small matters will eventually be entrusted with much more.

1 Thessalonians 4:9–11
Psalm 98
Matthew 25:14–30

AUGUST 28

Do not conform yourselves to this age but be transformed by the renewal of your mind, that you may discern what is the will of God, what is good and pleasing and perfect.

—ROMANS 12:2

Lord, I can't just follow the crowd, can I? The very philosophy that's at the core of my surrounding culture is at odds with your purposes. It's not enough to be "normal" or a "nice person." Please transform my mind and heart so that I am in tune with a higher reality.

Jeremiah 20:7–9
Psalm 63
Romans 12:1–2
Matthew 16:21–27

AUGUST 29

• THE MARTYRDOM OF SAINT JOHN THE BAPTIST •

Herod feared John, knowing him to be a righteous and holy man, and kept him in custody. When he heard him speak he was very much perplexed, yet he liked to listen to him.

—MARK 6:20

Herod's was a typical reaction to holiness. We are drawn to holiness yet afraid of what it might require of us. We resist being confronted about our sin yet want to hear more about it. Herod eventually executed John the Baptist by chopping off his head. We make choices every day that either bring God's holiness to life within us or kill it before it can have any effect.

1 Thessalonians 4:13–18
Psalm 71
Mark 6:17–29

For all of you are children of the light and children of the day. We are not of the night or of darkness. Therefore, let us not sleep as the rest do, but let us stay alert and sober.

—1 THESSALONIANS 5:5–6

We know how it feels to be in a "dark" place, where the emotional tone is hostile or fearful and where the conversation puts us on edge. It may be a party or someone's home, but we are relieved to get out of there. Our souls have tasted God's light. May we never again be comfortable in darkness.

1 Thessalonians 5:1–6, 9–11
Psalm 27
Luke 4:31–37

We always give thanks to God, the Father of our Lord Jesus Christ,
when we pray for you, for we have heard of your faith in Christ Jesus
and the love that you have for all the holy ones because of the hope
reserved for you in heaven.

—COLOSSIANS 1:3–5

I give thanks, God, for the many partners I have had on
my journey of faith. I give thanks for Sunday school
teachers, pastors, friends at school, colleagues in
ministry—every person who has demonstrated Christ's love
to me. May I not only give thanks for them but also
remember them by name in my prayers.

Colossians 1:1–8
Psalm 52
Luke 4:38–44

Jesus said to Simon, "Do not be afraid; from now on you will be catching men."

—LUKE 5:10

Simon the fisherman would now fish for people. Whatever you have done up to now, Jesus can transform those skills and abilities for use in God's kingdom. No knowledge or experience is wasted. Even in your less noble activities you have cultivated some quality that becomes beneficial under the influence of faith. What has life been preparing you to do?

Colossians 1:9–14
Psalm 98
Luke 5:1–11

[N]o one who has been drinking old wine desires new, for he says, "The old is good."

—LUKE 5:39

Jesus might have said, "You don't know what you're missing." If we've never had the good stuff, we think that what we have is good enough. Jesus urges us to consider that whatever we have is a lesser version of what God wants us to experience. Are we willing to look at our lives and say, "No, this really isn't good enough"? Do we dare to say, "I want something better"?

Colossians 1:15–20
Psalm 100
Luke 5:33–39

Saturday

SEPTEMBER 3

• SAINT GREGORY THE GREAT, POPE AND DOCTOR OF THE CHURCH •

[Y]ou who once were alienated and hostile in mind because of evil deeds he has now reconciled in his fleshly body through his death, to present you holy, without blemish, and irreproachable before him.

—COLOSSIANS 1:21–22

My actions do have an impact on my soul. It's as if every sin puts a mark on me and turns me a little more into a person of sin. Jesus somehow took upon himself all that damage, allowing me to be free of those marks. I can become holy now.

Colossians 1:21–23
Psalm 54
Luke 6:1–5

SEPTEMBER 4

You, son of man, I have appointed watchman for the house of Israel;
when you hear me say anything, you shall warn them for me.

—EZEKIEL 33:7

Daniel didn't want to meddle in Ed's affairs, but he recognized some behavior patterns in his friend that he knew would lead to danger and possibly to harm. He and Ed had been neighbors for several years; if Daniel didn't speak up, who would? When Daniel finally broached the subject (as tactfully as he could), Ed responded not in hostility but in relief—that someone would help him face his situation.

Ezekiel 33:7–9
Psalm 95
Romans 13:8–10
Matthew 18:15–20

My soul, be at rest in God alone,
from whom comes my hope.
God alone is my rock and my salvation,
my secure height; I shall not fall.

—PSALM 62:6-7

Sometimes we have to engage in some healthy self-talk: "My soul, be at rest in God alone." "My soul, remember that God is watching over you." "My soul, try to remember all the other times you felt like this and things worked out anyway." "My soul, you belong to God of the universe—do you really think God will allow you to fall?"

Colossians 1:24–2:3
Psalm 62
Luke 6:6–11

SEPTEMBER 6

See to it that no one captivate you with an empty, seductive philosophy according to human tradition, according to the elemental powers of the world and not according to Christ.

—COLOSSIANS 2:8

Haley was always being drawn to new systems that promised her a better life. With each new system, she joined a new group, learned their vocabulary, read their literature, and attached herself to their leader. A few months would pass, something would "go wrong," as she put it, and she'd hunt for a new answer. Not once did she consider that the Christian faith of her childhood might have something to offer.

Colossians 2:6–15
Psalm 145
Luke 6:12–19

*If then you were raised with Christ, seek what is above, where Christ is
seated at the right hand of God.*

—COLOSSIANS 3:1

Greg and Jennifer became Christians during their fifth year
of marriage. They already had routines, shared values, and
plans for what they wanted in life. But as they grew to
understand what it meant to be in Christ's fellowship, their
life together gradually changed. They had different desires
now, and different routines. Their plans for the future
changed, too. And they were more content and hopeful
than they'd been before.

Colossians 3:1–11
Psalm 145
Luke 6:20–26

SEPTEMBER 8

But you, Bethlehem-Ephrathah,
too small to be among the clans of Judah,
From you shall come forth for me
one who is to be ruler in Israel;
Whose origin is from of old,
from ancient times.

—MICAH 5:1

We never know the times or locations in which miracles
will happen. Not only did the Messiah come from an
insignificant place, but he also came "from ancient times."
Once again God demonstrates that past, present, and
future are conditions of a merely physical world. And we
are left marveling at all God has done throughout history
so that we can find grace today.

Micah 5:1–4 or Romans 8:28–30
Psalm 13
Matthew 1:1–16, 18–23 or 1:18–23

Why do you notice the splinter in your brother's eye, but do not perceive the wooden beam in your own?

—LUKE 6:41

Margaret's world turned upside down the day she overheard someone say, "Well, a person notices in others what she's guilty of herself." It wasn't a conversation about her, but she thought immediately of how often she listed her sister-in-law's bad habits. Just a moment's reflection revealed to Margaret that some of those habits were her own.

1 Timothy 1:1–2, 12–14
Psalm 16
Luke 6:39–42

*A good person out of the store of goodness in his heart produces good,
but an evil person out of a store of evil produces evil; for from the
fullness of the heart the mouth speaks.*

—LUKE 6:45

I'd like to believe that I'm a "different" person when driving
in heavy traffic, that the things I say to other drivers are
coming from another personality that shows up only in
that situation. But the truth is that all that anger is in me
regardless of the situation; it's simply more acceptable to
verbalize it in the privacy of my car. My words will always
reveal my heart.

1 Timothy 1:15–17
Psalm 113
Luke 6:43–49

Should a man nourish anger against his fellows
and expect healing from the LORD?
Should a man refuse mercy to his fellows,
yet seek pardon for his own sins?

—SIRACH 28:3–4

Lord, I have sometimes been the victim of double standards, and I don't want to be a part of such a system. Help me give others the mercy and understanding that I hope to receive from you.

Sirach 27:30–28:9
Psalm 103
Romans 14:7–9
Matthew 18:21–35

I did not consider myself worthy to come to you; but say the word and
let my servant be healed. For I too am a person subject to authority,
with soldiers subject to me. And I say to one, "Go," and he goes.

—LUKE 7:7–8

The centurion who is speaking understands that God's authority enables Jesus to simply say the word and make sickness flee. Jesus is impressed that someone outside of the Jewish community is able to recognize this. In our day-to-day experiences, do we consider how powerful our words are when we speak out of God's wisdom and will?

1 Timothy 2:1–8
Psalm 28
Luke 7:1–10

I look to the faithful of the land;
they alone can be my companions.
Those who follow the way of integrity,
they alone can enter my service.
—PSALM 101:6

Michael knew that he wasn't as qualified, technically, as the other job applicants. So he was surprised when the director hired him. "Mike, I know you'll have to learn some things on the job," he said, "but a person's character is as important as his skills. And you have already exhibited integrity and self-awareness, two traits that are crucial to the health of this company."

1 Timothy 3:1–13
Psalm 101
Luke 7:11–17

[H]e emptied himself,
taking the form of a slave,
coming in human likeness;
and found human in appearance,
he humbled himself,
becoming obedient to death,
even death on a cross.

—PHILIPPIANS 2:7–8

Because of Jesus' death on a cross, the cross has become holy to us. When Jesus came in human likeness, he made *being human* holy as well. His journey through this life prepared a way for us. We can come to each new day aware that we, too, are holy.

Numbers 21:4–9
Psalm 78
Philippians 2:6–11
John 3:13–17

SEPTEMBER 15

Let no one have contempt for your youth, but set an example for those who believe, in speech, conduct, love, faith, and purity. . . . Do not neglect the gift you have, which was conferred on you through the prophetic word with the imposition of hands of the presbyterate.
—1 TIMOTHY 4:12, 14

You may be young (or old, or sick, or poor), but as a person of faith, you have the means to do good, because God has given you specific gifts for the good of others and yourself. If the apostle Paul were writing this letter to you now, he would probably include the phrase "Go for it!"

1 Timothy 4:12–16
Psalm 31
John 19:25–27 or Luke 2:33–35

Friday

SEPTEMBER 16

• SAINT CORNELIUS, POPE AND MARTYR •
• SAINT CYPRIAN, BISHOP AND MARTYR •

Accompanying him were the Twelve and some women who had been cured of evil spirits and infirmities . . . who provided for them out of their resources.

—LUKE 8:1–3

How appropriate that this bit of information is included in the Gospel. Women were fairly invisible in the time of Jesus, but Luke took care to mention their constant presence in the Lord's ministry. Throughout the world, many women continue to be persecuted, oppressed, and silenced. Pray for them today, and thank God for those women who have loved and supported you.

1 Timothy 6:2–12
Psalm 49
Luke 8:1–3

When a large crowd gathered, with people from one town after another journeying to him, he spoke in a parable.

—LUKE 8:4

If you suddenly had the attention of people from all over your region of the country, what would you say? Would you tell cryptic stories that you later had to translate to a chosen few? That's what Jesus did. It is wisdom and the leading of God that tells us what to say and do when we would otherwise be tempted to jump at obvious opportunities. Jesus was looking for disciples, not merely mass approval.

1 Timothy 6:13–16
Psalm 100
Luke 8:4–15

[C]onduct yourselves in a way worthy of the gospel of Christ, so that, whether I come and see you or am absent, I may hear news of you, that you are standing firm in one spirit, with one mind struggling together for the faith of the gospel.

—PHILIPPIANS 1:27

Out of the blue, Clare received a letter from Judy, a high school classmate she had not been in touch with in twenty years. Clare had unknowingly talked with Judy's niece on a flight between Chicago and New Orleans, and something Clare had said to the young woman helped her hold on to faith during a difficult time. In the letter, Judy thanked Clare for her help. News of our faith will travel farther than we think.

Isaiah 55:6–9
Psalm 145
Philippians 1:20–24, 27
Matthew 20:1–16

Let everyone who has survived, in whatever place he may have dwelt, be assisted by the people of that place with silver, gold, goods, and cattle, together with free-will offerings for the house of God in Jerusalem.

—EZRA 1:4

Lord, as long as I walk with you, I will be more than just a survivor. Your grace will take me beyond survival to a life fully restored.

Ezra 1:1–6
Psalm 126
Luke 8:16–18

Tuesday

SEPTEMBER 20

• SAINTS ANDREW KIM TAEGON, PRIEST AND MARTYR, AND PAUL CHONG
HASANG, MARTYR, AND THEIR COMPANIONS, MARTYRS •

He was told, "Your mother and your brothers are standing outside and
they wish to see you." He said to them in reply, "My mother and my
brothers are those who hear the word of God and act on it."

—LUKE 8:20–21

Liz never foresaw how far God's grace would take her—or
how few people would travel at her side. The friends and
family members to whom she had always been so close
could not quite relate to her compassion for the poor or
her devotion to the sacraments. Yet God gave her new
companions, many of them from segments of society that
had been foreign to Liz in earlier times. She had entered a
new family altogether.

Ezra 6:7–8, 12, 14–20
Psalm 122
Luke 8:19–21

[H]e gave some as apostles, others as prophets, others as evangelists, others as pastors and teachers, to equip the holy ones for the work of ministry, for building up the body of Christ.

—EPHESIANS 4:11–12

You may not think of yourself as a gifted person, but God has given you abilities that are designed to build up the body of Christ. What are your gifts? And what opportunities to nurture others are right in front of you now?

Ephesians 4:1–7, 11–13
Psalm 19
Matthew 9:9–13

Thursday

SEPTEMBER 22

*Sing to the LORD a new song,
a hymn in the assembly of the faithful.*

—PSALM 149:1

There will always be fresh versions of eternal truths. They wait for us to discover and voice them. Part of our task, as worshipers of God, is to find new ways to describe God's presence to one another.

Haggai 1:1–8
Psalm 149
Luke 9:7–9

———————

Mine is the silver and mine the gold,
says the LORD of hosts.
Greater will be the future glory of this house
than the former, says the LORD of hosts.

—HAGGAI 2:8–9

God, I have no need to worry about resources when I'm
doing your work. Help me trust you more to make possible
all that you've given me to do.

Haggai 2:1–9
Psalm 43
Luke 9:18–22

*[T]hey did not understand this saying; its meaning was hidden from
them so that they should not understand it, and they were afraid to ask
him about this saying.*

—LUKE 9:45

Why would God hide from anyone the meaning of Jesus'
sayings? Perhaps there is a time for wondering. Perhaps
searching for understanding is itself an important aspect of
the faith process. And sometimes a person is not ready to
understand spiritual concepts—could it be that God hides
knowledge from us in order to protect us while we are
immature?

Zechariah 2:5–9, 14–15
Jeremiah 31:10–13
Luke 9:43–45

[I]f a wicked man, turning from the wickedness he has committed, does what is right and just, he shall preserve his life; since he has turned away from all the sins which he committed, he shall surely live, he shall not die.

—EZEKIEL 18:27–28

You will always have the power to make good choices for yourself. They will not always be easy choices, but they will be possible. And, as the prophet Ezekiel reminds us, God pays attention when we change our ways.

Ezekiel 18:25–28
Psalm 25
Philippians 2:1–11 or 2:1–5
Matthew 21:28–32

Of old you laid the earth's foundations;
the heavens are the work of your hands.
They perish, but you remain;
they all wear out like a garment; . . .
but you are the same, your years have no end.

—PSALM 102:26–28

We are reminded of how ephemeral humans are when we look at a mountain range that has stood for thousands, if not millions, of years. We see the weather and the seasons change, but we are confident that the solar system will stay in place until long after we're gone. What happens, then, when the mountains disappear and the sun burns itself out? Our God will still be God, and we will still be held safe in divine love.

Zechariah 8:1–8
Psalm 102
Luke 9:46–50

SEPTEMBER 27

• SAINT VINCENT DE PAUL, PRIEST •

Many peoples and strong nations shall come to seek the LORD of hosts
in Jerusalem and to implore the favor of the LORD.

—ZECHARIAH 8:22

The whole world is headed, ultimately, for Jerusalem, for
true worship of God. This is hard to believe when we see
the chaos of world events. That's why God's word is given
to us, to offer us a vision of hope.

Zechariah 8:20–23
Psalm 87
Luke 9:51–56

• SAINT LAWRENCE RUIZ AND HIS COMPANIONS, MARTYRS •
SAINT WENCESLAUS, MARTYR •

The king granted my requests, for the favoring hand of my God
was upon me.
—NEHEMIAH 2:8

There was no way the motion would be passed by city
council; most of its members were opposed to drug
rehabilitation programs being housed in the neighborhood.
But God-fearing people gathered in their churches,
mosques, and synagogues and prayed for God's mercy and
justice. The motion did pass, and despite the self-
congratulatory speeches of council members, those who
had prayed knew that God's hand was in it.

Nehemiah 2:1–8
Psalm 137
Luke 9:57–62

Then war broke out in heaven; Michael and his angels battled against the dragon. The dragon and its angels fought back, but they did not prevail and there was no longer any place for them in heaven.

—REVELATION 12:7–8

Whether we take this passage literally or figuratively, we can appreciate the truth it reveals: conflict between good and evil is a reality. We are engaged in the conflict in daily life, but it exists also in dimensions we cannot understand. Even if we don't believe in angels, we can believe that God's power is on our side in the battle and that ultimately good will win.

Daniel 7:9–10, 13–14 or Revelation 12:7–12
Psalm 138
John 1:47–51

Justice is with the LORD, our God; and we today are flushed with shame, we men of Judah and citizens of Jerusalem, that we, with our kings and rulers and priests and prophets, and with our fathers, have sinned in the LORD's sight and disobeyed him.

—BARUCH 1:15–18

Have you noticed that wrongdoing nearly always involves more than just one person or segment of society? The Israelites acknowledged that all parts of their population had sinned against God: citizens, rulers, priests, and prophets. When we accuse our politicians, clergy, or military leaders of doing wrong, we have to ask how we, too, have participated.

Baruch 1:15–22
Psalm 79
Luke 10:13–16

• SAINT THÉRÈSE OF THE CHILD JESUS,
VIRGIN AND DOCTOR OF THE CHURCH •

*[D]o not rejoice because the spirits are subject to you, but rejoice
because your names are written in heaven.*

—LUKE 10:20

Lord, I long for power and wisdom, for others to respect
my gifts, for a prayer life that is "effective." Help me see
myself today as simply your child, whose name is written
in heaven, whose life is in your hands, and whose value
does not depend on anything but your love.

Baruch 4:5–12, 27–29
Psalm 69
Luke 10:17–24

Sunday

OCTOBER 2

LORD of hosts,
how long will you burn with anger
while your people pray?
You have fed them the bread of tears,
made them drink tears in abundance.

—PSALM 80:5–6

Why don't we pray like this anymore? We try to rationalize suffering by explaining how God will "use" it to help us. The people of Israel cried out in brutal honesty and asked God point-blank, "How long will you let this go on?" Maybe God wants us to get honest, to cry out, to demand an answer. Maybe this kind of prayer is necessary to the growth of our souls.

Isaiah 5:1–7
Psalm 80
Philippians 4:6–9
Matthew 21:33–43

Monday

OCTOBER 3

*This is the word of the LORD that came to Jonah . . . : "Set out for
the great city of Nineveh, and preach against it; their wickedness has
come up before me." But Jonah made ready to flee to Tarshish, away
from the LORD.*

—JONAH 1:1–3

If you talk to enough people, you will discover that there
are a lot of Jonahs in our midst—people who have heard
God's voice and have promptly run in the other direction.
Maybe you're a Jonah, too? At this very moment, are you
walking alongside God? Or is your life a pattern of
avoidance?

Jonah 1:1–2:2, 11
Psalm 2
Luke 10:25–37

Jonah began his journey through the city, and had gone but a single day's walk announcing, "Forty days more and Nineveh shall be destroyed," when the people of Nineveh believed God; they proclaimed a fast and all of them, great and small, put on sackcloth.

—JONAH 3:4–5

Phil expected to be laughed out of the room when he began to explain the church's teaching on sexuality to his friend Derick. Derick was hardly sexually discreet, but he had asked about the subject and became uncharacteristically sober while Phil talked. Suddenly he confessed to Phil the damage he had caused in several relationships. "I want to clean up my act," he said.

Jonah 3:1–10
Psalm 130
Luke 10:38–42

OCTOBER 5

He was praying in a certain place, and when he had finished, one of his disciples said to him, "Lord, teach us to pray just as John taught his disciples."

—LUKE 11:1

Evelyn was possibly the wisest person Amanda had ever met, and she had much experience with prayer, meditation, and other spiritual disciplines that Amanda was still trying to learn. It took awhile for Amanda to work up the courage, but one day she asked Evelyn if she might help her develop some good soul habits. Evelyn graciously said yes, and Amanda's new journey began.

Jonah 4:1–11
Psalm 86
Luke 11:1–4

[A]sk and you will receive; seek and you will find; knock and the door will be opened to you. For everyone who asks, receives; and the one who seeks, finds; and to the one who knocks, the door will be opened.

—LUKE 11:9–10

Jesus, you have issued such a direct and specific invitation to me. You want me to come to you for what I need. You want me to have dreams and hopes and to involve you as I seek them. Help me to be bold and to ask and seek and knock. Help me walk through my life expecting good things and looking for your provision.

Malachi 3:13–20
Psalm 1
Luke 11:5–13

Friday

OCTOBER 7

• OUR LADY OF THE ROSARY •

The nations fall into the pit they dig;
in the snare they hide, their own foot is caught.
The LORD is revealed in this divine rule:
by the deeds they do the wicked are trapped.

—PSALM 9:16–17

Freedom is not the ability to do whatever we want and get away with it—as the psalmist shows, evildoers are trapped by their own evil acts. It is better to view freedom as the ability to refrain from harming others or ourselves.

Joel 1:13–15; 2:1–2
Psalm 9
Luke 11:15–26

[A] woman from the crowd called out and said to him, "Blessed is the womb that carried you and the breasts at which you nursed." He replied, "Rather, blessed are those who hear the word of God and observe it."

—LUKE 11:27–28

No one could accuse Jesus of being sentimental. A woman tried to gush over him, and he stopped her cold. Always he guided people back to what was most important. Were they listening to God? Were they doing what they knew they should be doing? Did their lives match their words? He asks the same questions of you and me.

Joel 4:12–21
Psalm 97
Luke 11:27–28

On this mountain the LORD of hosts
will provide for all peoples
A feast of rich food and choice wines. . . .
On this mountain he will destroy
the veil that veils all peoples,
The web that is woven over all nations;
he will destroy death forever.

—ISAIAH 25:6–8

All you have to do is watch the news to understand "the web that is woven over all nations." We live as if a heavy veil blinds us to injustice and suffering. Let us pray that God keeps lifting the veil and freeing us from the web that traps us.

Isaiah 25:6–10
Psalm 23
Philippians 4:12–14, 19–20
Matthew 22:1–14 or 22:1–10

*Just as Jonah became a sign to the Ninevites, so will the Son of Man be
to this generation.*
—LUKE 11:30

Harold is confined to a wheelchair, the result of his violent
days as a gang member. He's been out of that lifestyle for
several years now, but he makes a point to be on the streets
often, in his still-dangerous neighborhood. When people
ask why he puts himself in harm's way, he says, "I'm a sign
to the kids around here. They see this wheelchair, and they
see me, and they understand how I got here. If my
presence helps one kid stay out of the gangs, I've done a
good thing."

Romans 1:1–7
Psalm 98
Luke 11:29–32

Tuesday

OCTOBER 11

The wrath of God is indeed being revealed from heaven against every impiety and wickedness of those who suppress the truth by their wickedness. For what can be known about God is evident to them, because God made it evident to them.

—ROMANS 1:18–19

I cannot understand the inner workings of others' lives. But I can trust that God makes the truth evident to every person in some way and at some time (probably many times). And I can take care never to suppress the truth. It could be that by allowing the truth to shine in my life, I'll give others courage to do the same.

Romans 1:16–25
Psalm 19
Luke 11:37–41

Woe also to you scholars of the law! You impose on people burdens hard to carry, but you yourselves do not lift one finger to touch them.

—LUKE 11:46

God holds teachers accountable for how their teaching affects people. In this case, Jesus reprimands religious teachers for oppressing the people by making God's law impossible to carry out. Teaching that is holy guides people into God's embrace.

Romans 2:1–11
Psalm 62
Luke 11:42–46

OCTOBER 13

Does God belong to Jews alone? Does he not belong to Gentiles, too?
Yes, also to Gentiles, for God is one and will justify the circumcised on
the basis of faith and the uncircumcised through faith.

—ROMANS 3:29–30

Lord, when I am feeling too confident about my faith,
my church, my practices and beliefs, remind me that you
are working through all people of faith everywhere and
that it's not my job to judge whom you "belong" to and
whom you don't.

Romans 3:21–30
Psalm 130
Luke 11:47–54

A worker's wage is credited not as a gift, but as something due. But when one does not work, yet believes in the one who justifies the ungodly, his faith is credited as righteousness.

—ROMANS 4:4–5

"For his lenient attitude toward repentant sinners he incurred the wrath of the rigorists." Thus one reference book comments on St. Callistus, who apparently took to heart Paul's words in the letter to the Romans. We do not earn righteousness—we can only believe in God, and this is righteousness enough.

Romans 4:1–8
Psalm 32
Luke 12:1–7

Saturday

OCTOBER 15

• SAINT TERESA OF JESUS, VIRGIN AND DOCTOR OF THE CHURCH •

Rely on the mighty LORD;
constantly seek his face.
Recall the wondrous deeds he has done,
his signs and his words of judgment.

—PSALM 105:4–5

After months of no prospects, a wonderful opportunity appears. After weeks of struggling in a relationship, a breakthrough happens. After drought and weariness, the rains come. Life gives us one example after another of God's wondrous deeds and care for us.

Romans 4:13, 16–18
Psalm 105
Luke 12:8–12

OCTOBER 16

[O]ur gospel did not come to you in word alone, but also in power and in the holy Spirit and [with] much conviction.

—1 THESSALONIANS 1:5

Although he'd been through years of religious schooling, Tony found it impossible to believe in God. Then one day in the grocery store he saw an elderly gentleman drop a jar of mayonnaise. Tony helped clean it up, and the gentleman grasped his arm, looked into his eyes, and said, "God bless and keep you, son." The words echoed in Tony's head all the way home, and he felt a loving presence all around him. That was the beginning of his belief.

Isaiah 45:1, 4–6
Psalm 96
1 Thessalonians 1:1–5
Matthew 22:15–21

Then [Jesus] said to the crowd, "Take care to guard against all greed, for though one may be rich, one's life does not consist of possessions."

—LUKE 12:15

If I suddenly lost all my things, what would I do? If I could save just a few things from a fire or flood, what would they be? If I had to wander for a year with just a backpack, what would I take? How much of my emotional life is taken up with concern for my possessions?

Romans 4:20–25
Luke 1:69–75
Luke 12:13–21

OCTOBER 18

• SAINT LUKE, EVANGELIST •

At my first defense no one appeared on my behalf, but everyone deserted me. . . . But the Lord stood by me and gave me strength, so that through me the proclamation might be completed and all the Gentiles might hear it. And I was rescued from the lion's mouth.

—2 TIMOTHY 4:16–17

William had always turned to others for help—to his pastor, a favorite teacher, the youth director, his best friend. Then he went through a series of crises when, for one reason or another, none of his "support team" was available. For the first time William had to trust in God alone. God indeed provided the grace needed, and William's faith grew dramatically during that time.

2 Timothy 4:10–17
Psalm 145
Luke 10:1–9

Do you not know that if you present yourselves to someone as obedient slaves, you are slaves of the one you obey, either of sin, which leads to death, or of obedience, which leads to righteousness?

—ROMANS 6:16

Bob Dylan recorded a song years ago called "Gotta Serve Somebody." We have to make a choice: will we serve God or someone else? Even if we serve ourselves, we remove ourselves from God's service—and regardless of our intentions, we often end up pleasing our base desires. In serving God, who loves us, we ultimately serve ourselves best, and the world as well.

Romans 6:12–18
Psalm 124
Luke 12:39–48

Thursday

OCTOBER 20

• SAINT PAUL OF THE CROSS, PRIEST •

[N]ow that you have been freed from sin and have become slaves of God, the benefit that you have leads to sanctification, and its end is eternal life. For the wages of sin is death, but the gift of God is eternal life in Christ Jesus our Lord.

—ROMANS 6:22–23

I'd like to think that I'm completely free to do and be whatever I want. But in fact I am not free until I give my life completely to God. And all the good things I can work to get for myself hardly compare with the good gifts God has for me.

Romans 6:19–23
Psalm 1
Luke 12:49–53

*I discover the principle that when I want to do right, evil is at hand.
For I take delight in the law of God, in my inner self, but I see in my
members another principle at war with the law of my mind, taking me
captive to the law of sin that dwells in my members.*

—ROMANS 7:21–23

Who can't relate to Paul's dilemma? We know what we
should do, but we don't do it. It's as if we've got a whole
other person inside us, arguing and making excuses. We
can do what Paul did: call this conflict sin and confess it.
That's a good beginning to transforming ourselves from the
inside out.

Romans 7:18–25
Psalm 119
Luke 12:54–59

[N]ow there is no condemnation for those who are in Christ Jesus. For the law of the spirit of life in Christ Jesus has freed you from the law of sin and death.

—ROMANS 8:1–2

Imagine that you've committed a crime punishable by death, yet the judge declares that you are free to go. Your record does not indicate the crime at all. This image gives us an idea of God's generosity toward us. We are no longer condemned. Our life in Christ has placed us in a different reality entirely.

Romans 8:1–11
Psalm 24
Luke 13:1–9

OCTOBER 23

You shall not molest or oppress an alien, for you were once aliens yourselves in the land of Egypt. You shall not wrong any widow or orphan. If ever you wrong them and they cry out to me, I will surely hear their cry.

—EXODUS 22:20–22

Are you a stranger in a new land? Are you alone in the world? If so, God is looking out for you.

Exodus 22:20–26
Psalm 18
1 Thessalonians 1:5–10
Matthew 22:34–40

[Y]ou did not receive a spirit of slavery to fall back into fear, but you received a spirit of adoption, through which we cry, "Abba, Father!"

—ROMANS 8:15

Sharon walked away from faith when she was fourteen. Years of trying to please an angry god had exhausted her. At age thirty-two, Sharon discovered that what she had worshiped had not been God at all but the invention of a religious culture that controlled people through fear of punishment. Sharon sensed her soul responding to the embrace of divine love and knew that she had met the true God at last.

Romans 8:12–17
Psalm 68
Luke 13:10–17

OCTOBER 25

*I consider that the sufferings of this present time are as nothing
compared with the glory to be revealed for us.*

—ROMANS 8:18

It's good to live in the present. In fact, it's usually best to
accept our situation and work within it rather than try to
escape it. But sometimes it is entirely appropriate to look
ahead to the life beyond this one. When our suffering is
great we can focus on our eternal future with God, when
the troubles of this life will fall away.

Romans 8:18–25
Psalm 126
Luke 13:18–21

Wednesday

OCTOBER 26

How long, LORD? Will you utterly forget me?
How long will you hide your face from me?
How long must I carry sorrow in my soul,
grief in my heart day after day?
How long will my enemy triumph over me?

—PSALM 13:2–3

Yes, there are times when God's face is completely hidden,
when a person feels utterly forgotten and the soul is
burdened with sorrow. The psalmist does not apologize for
feeling bad or for being a wimp. Rather, he cries out to
God, and his prayer is full of questions. Sometimes
questions are all a person can offer to God.

Romans 8:26–30
Psalm 13
Luke 13:22–30

*If God is for us, who can be against us? He who did not spare his own
Son but handed him over for us all, how will he not also give us
everything else along with him?*

—ROMANS 8:31–32

Today, repeat this question many times: If God is for me,
who can be against me?

Romans 8:31–39
Psalm 109
Luke 13:31–35

[Y]ou are no longer strangers and sojourners, but you are fellow citizens with the holy ones and members of the household of God, built upon the foundation of the apostles and prophets, with Christ Jesus himself as the capstone.

—EPHESIANS 2:19–20

Anyone who has traveled knows how it feels to be weary and hungry in unfamiliar surroundings. And then a door opens and there's a friendly face, and you are brought in and fed and given a place to clean up and a cozy bed. The world suddenly feels different; it has become home. This is what happens to us when we come to faith in Christ. We are gathered into God's home and find a whole family waiting for us.

Ephesians 2:19–22
Psalm 19
Luke 6:12–16

OCTOBER 29

[E]veryone who exalts himself will be humbled, but the one who humbles himself will be exalted.

—LUKE 14:11

The life of faith is in many ways diametrically opposed to earthly life. From an earthly point of view, life is a constant exercise in gaining control and prestige in order to get what we want. From the viewpoint of faith, we gain in every way by giving of ourselves entirely with no thought to our position or power. The challenge is to ask ourselves regularly, "Am I grasping, or am I giving?"

Romans 11:1–2, 11–12, 25–29
Psalm 94
Luke 14:1, 7–11

Sunday

OCTOBER 30

• DAYLIGHT SAVING TIME ENDS •

Have we not all the one Father?
Has not the one God created us?
Why then do we break faith with each other,
violating the covenant of our fathers?

—MALACHI 2:10

Years ago I visited Jerusalem. The words of the prophet Malachi could not be more appropriate to another place in the world. I saw the ruins of the Jewish temple, the Muslims' Dome of the Rock, and several Christian sites, such as the Garden of Gethsemane and the Church of the Annunciation. All three faiths honor the God of Abraham, yet they have continued to war against one another. May our religious leaders heed the prophet's cry.

Malachi 1:14–2:2, 8–10
Psalm 131
1 Thessalonians 2:7–9, 13
Matthew 23:1–12

———

⇒ 339 ⇐

[W]hen you hold a banquet, invite the poor, the crippled, the lame, the blind; blessed indeed will you be because of their inability to repay you. For you will be repaid at the resurrection of the righteous.

—LUKE 14:13–14

Lord, I am afraid to open my doors to the poor and sick. What if I can't care for them all? What if we run out of food? What if they need me too much? Help me be faithful enough to leave these questions with you and simply do what you say.

Romans 11:29–36
Psalm 69
Luke 14:12–14

After this I had a vision of a great multitude, which no one could count,
from every nation, race, people, and tongue. They stood before the
throne and before the Lamb, wearing white robes and holding palm
branches in their hands.

—REVELATION 7:9

The mission conference offered a glimpse of what heaven must look like. Music swelled the hall as people processed down both aisles of the auditorium. They came from more than forty countries and wore traditional costumes of their cultures. For the invocation, the group said the Lord's Prayer together. Words of many languages mixed in the air, and light shone out of every possible face, body type, and skin tone.

Revelation 7:2–4, 9–14
Psalm 24
1 John 3:1–3
Matthew 5:1–12

[T]he souls of the just are in the hand of God,
and no torment shall touch them.
They seemed, in the view of the foolish, to be dead;
and their passing away was thought an affliction
and their going forth from us, utter destruction.
But they are in peace.

—WISDOM 3:1–3

Yes, Lord, death seems so final to us on earth. It feels as if we have reached the end of everything. The loss of physical life is devastating, and we can barely perceive any other reality. What a comfort to know that our souls rest peacefully in your hands.

Wisdom 3:1–9
Psalm 27 or 103
Romans 5:5–11 or 6:3–9
John 6:37–40 or any readings taken from the Masses for the Dead, nos. 1011–1016

None of us lives for oneself, and no one dies for oneself. For if we live,
we live for the Lord, and if we die, we die for the Lord; so then, whether
we live or die, we are the Lord's.

—ROMANS 14:7–8

Lord Jesus, help me see my life as held within yours. If I
believe that I am yours no matter what, I won't be
motivated by greed or fear.

Romans 14:7–12
Psalm 27
Luke 15:1–10

I aspire to proclaim the gospel not where Christ has already been named, so that I do not build on another's foundation.

—ROMANS 15:20

Paul was so sure of his particular calling that he was careful to draw boundaries for himself. He would do the work God called him to do, no more and no less. May each of us be discerning enough to learn God's will and disciplined enough to follow it completely.

Romans 15:14–21
Psalm 98
Luke 16:1–8

The eyes of all look hopefully to you;
you give them their food in due season.
You open wide your hand
and satisfy the desire of every living thing.

—PSALM 145:15–16

Teri noticed that the more Sonny, her German shepherd, learned to trust her, the calmer he became. As Sonny gazed at her expectantly, Teri realized how much power she had simply because she gave him everything he needed. It was a humbling experience. Teri hoped she could learn to trust God a bit more, the One who provided for her. Perhaps increased trust could help Teri be calmer, too.

Romans 16:3–9, 16, 22–27
Psalm 145
Luke 16:9–15

NOVEMBER 6

We do not want you to be unaware, brothers, about those who have fallen asleep, so that you may not grieve like the rest, who have no hope. For if we believe that Jesus died and rose, so too will God, through Jesus, bring with him those who have fallen asleep.

—1 THESSALONIANS 4:13–14

Lord, you've given us such straightforward assurance. Because Jesus rose from the dead, so will we. Although it is a mystery, the fact is a simple one. Help us hold on to these words, and allow this hope to shape every day of our lives.

Wisdom 6:12–16
Psalm 63
1 Thessalonians 4:13–18 or 4:13–14
Matthew 25:1–13

*He said to his disciples, "Things that cause sin will inevitably occur,
but woe to the person through whom they occur. . . . Be on your guard!
If your brother sins, rebuke him; and if he repents, forgive him."*

—LUKE 17:1, 3

It seems that I am indeed responsible for my brothers,
sisters, friends, and neighbors. We have to watch out for
one another, because, well, sin happens. We have to be
willing to speak up and identify sin when it comes along.
And we must help one another move ahead by offering
forgiveness.

Wisdom 1:1–7
Psalm 139
Luke 17:1–6

For God formed man to be imperishable;
the image of his own nature he made him.
But by the envy of the devil, death entered the world,
and they who are in his possession experience it.
—WISDOM 2:23–24

When my father died, I was surprised at how wrong it felt.
He had been ill for a long time, and he seemed spiritually
ready to meet God. But it felt like such a mistake, such an
act against nature. The writer of these Wisdom verses
pinpoints the issue: we were designed never to perish.
Death entered the human situation because of evil. So my
instincts were right after all. Death was never God's
intention for us.

Wisdom 2:23–3:9
Psalm 34
Luke 17:7–10

Do you not know that you are the temple of God, and that the Spirit of God dwells in you?

—1 CORINTHIANS 3:16

Holy Spirit, create in each of us a spacious heart in which to house you, a healthy body in which to carry you, and a discerning mind with which to understand you.

Ezekiel 47:1–2, 8–9, 12
Psalm 84
1 Corinthians 3:9–11, 16–17
John 2:13–22

For Wisdom is mobile beyond all motion,
and she penetrates and pervades all things by reason of her purity. . . .
And passing into holy souls from age to age,
she produces friends of God and prophets.

—WISDOM 7:24, 27

We enjoy people who make us laugh. We depend on people who are strong. We are attracted to people who are gentle with us. But those who are truly wise bring us the ultimate comfort and security, because we sense that they commune directly with God.

Wisdom 7:22–8:1
Psalm 119
Luke 17:20–25

For all men were by nature foolish who were in ignorance of God, and who from the good things seen did not succeed in knowing him who is, and from studying the works did not discern the artisan.

—WISDOM 13:1

Many artists and scientists find God not through religious training but through their own work. The artist eventually recognizes the God behind beauty and inspiration, and the scientist eventually concludes that Someone designed the fantastic universe being studied. God becomes apparent when we are open to seeing "him who is."

Wisdom 13:1–9
Psalm 19
Luke 17:26–37

Then [Jesus] told them a parable about the necessity for them to pray always without becoming weary.

—LUKE 18:1

The parable Jesus tells is about a widow who pesters a wicked judge until he finally gives her justice. The point? If a wicked judge can be swayed by persistence, how much more a holy God? Thanks to this humorous example, we know that we can never pray too much.

Wisdom 18:14–16; 19:6–9
Psalm 105
Luke 18:1–8

NOVEMBER 13

Charm is deceptive and beauty fleeting;
the woman who fears the LORD is to be praised.
Give her a reward of her labors,
and let her works praise her at the city gates.

—PROVERBS 31:30–31

When these words were written, most matters of importance were conducted at the city gates, whether business transactions or family agreements. How refreshing that a woman is seen here as a person of substance, one of faith and good works, one who is not defined by her appearance. She takes her place in the community and is praised for her labor.

Proverbs 31:10–13, 19–20, 30–31
Psalm 128
1 Thessalonians 5:1–6
Matthew 25:14–30 or 25:14–15, 19–21

NOVEMBER 14

*In those days there appeared in Israel men who were breakers of the law,
and they seduced many people, saying: "Let us go and make an alliance
with the Gentiles all around us; since we separated from them, many
evils have come upon us." . . . They covered over the mark of their
circumcision and abandoned the holy covenant; they allied themselves
with the Gentiles and sold themselves to wrongdoing.*

—1 MACCABEES 1:11, 15

Can I embrace wholeheartedly my heritage? Did my
forebearers embrace it? Did we change things about
ourselves in order to blend in more readily, or did we
abandon practices of faith because they made us seem
strange? Do I embrace my spiritual heritage as a child of
God? Do I place myself firmly in the community of faith?

1 Maccabees 1:10–15, 41–43, 54–57, 62–63
Psalm 119
Luke 18:35–43

Tuesday

NOVEMBER 15

• SAINT ALBERT THE GREAT, BISHOP AND DOCTOR OF THE CHURCH •

Whenever I lay down and slept,
the LORD preserved me to rise again.
I do not fear, then, thousands of people
arrayed against me on every side.

—PSALM 3:6–7

We can obsess over the world's dangers and thus live in fear. Or we can give thanks every morning we wake up. This gratitude has little to do with actual safety—the psalmist slept well even when surrounded by enemies. We should recall this image when we're tempted to lie awake at night worrying about what might happen tomorrow. Better to simply give thanks when tomorrow comes.

2 Maccabees 6:18–31
Psalm 3
Luke 19:1–10

⋛ 355 ⋚

Most admirable and worthy of everlasting remembrance was the mother,
who saw her seven sons perish in a single day, yet bore it courageously
because of her hope in the LORD.

—2 MACCABEES 7:20

Heavenly Father, for mothers throughout the world today
who must watch their children die, we ask your utmost
grace, peace, and courage.

2 Maccabees 7:1, 20–31
Psalm 17
Luke 19:11–28

Many who sought to live according to righteousness and religious custom went out into the desert to settle there.

—1 MACCABEES 2:29

The only job Jennifer could find was in a small town that was far from her former life in every way. She started attending church again because it was the town's only social outlet. But the solitude of her home and the familiarity of the liturgy led Jennifer back to a self she had forgotten. She realized how starved her soul had been. When she returned to the city two years later, she felt healed and whole.

1 Maccabees 2:15–29
Psalm 50
Luke 19:41–44

Friday

NOVEMBER 18

• THE DEDICATION OF THE BASILICAS OF SAINTS PETER AND PAUL,
APOSTLES, IN ROME • SAINT ROSE-PHILIPPINE DUCHESNE, VIRGIN •

On the anniversary of the day on which the Gentiles had defiled [the altar], on that very day it was reconsecrated with songs, harps, flutes, and cymbals.

—1 MACCABEES 4:54

After her home was robbed, Lana found it difficult to keep living there. Finally, she invited friends, family, and members of her church to the house, and they spent a Sunday afternoon blessing every room. They lit candles, and church musicians played. They asked the Holy Spirit to heal painful memories, and they ended with a feast. When the celebration was over, Lana had reclaimed her home.

1 Maccabees 4:36–37, 52–59
1 Chronicles 29:10–12
Luke 19:45–48
or (for the memorial of the dedication):
Acts 28:11–16, 30–31
Psalm 98
Matthew 14:22–33

NOVEMBER 19

That the dead will rise even Moses made known in the passage about the bush, when he called "Lord" the God of Abraham, the God of Isaac, and the God of Jacob; and he is not God of the dead, but of the living, for to him all are alive.

—LUKE 20:37–38

When three of his family members died within a year, Jonathon had to face his beliefs about life and death. Questions would jolt him awake at night: *Is this physical existence all there is? Is it possible that my loved ones no longer exist? Am I willing to write them off now? Or does the soul keep living?* Jonathon's questioning and reflection led him to a deeper understanding of life and death. Thus the season of grief became a season of new faith.

1 Maccabees 6:1–13
Psalm 9
Luke 20:27–40

When the Son of Man comes in his glory, and all the angels with him,
he will sit upon his glorious throne, and all the nations will be
assembled before him. And he will separate them one from another, as a
shepherd separates the sheep from the goats.

—MATTHEW 25:31–32

Yes, there will be a time of judgment. We know very little about it, but the important fact is this: Jesus himself, who is both God and man, will gaze upon every nation and will speak the utter truth.

Ezekiel 34:11–12, 15–17
Psalm 23
1 Corinthians 15:20–26, 28
Matthew 25:31–46

To these four young men God gave knowledge and proficiency in all literature and science, and to Daniel the understanding of all visions and dreams.

—DANIEL 1:17

Jason considered entering the ministry because he wanted to enrich people's spiritual lives. But his gifts lay in the sciences, leading him first into research and finally into a teaching position at a foremost university. Students sought out Jason for help with their projects—and to talk about faith. As Jason marveled at the spiritual hunger in these students, he saw that his abilities had placed him right where God needed him.

Daniel 1:1–6, 8–20
Daniel 3:52–56
Luke 21:1–4

While some people were speaking about how the temple was adorned with costly stones and votive offerings, he said, "All that you see here— the days will come when there will not be left a stone upon another stone that will not be thrown down."

—LUKE 21:5–6

Jesus never allowed people to get comfortable. Just as they were taking pleasure in the riches of God's temple, he reminded them that it was just a building and that someday it would be gone. What do you suppose Jesus would say to you if he wanted to remind you of what is most important in life? What might he say to disturb your comfort zone?

Daniel 2:31–45
Daniel 3:57–61
Luke 21:5–11

Then Daniel was brought into the presence of the king. The king asked him, "Are you the Daniel, the Jewish exile, whom my father, the king, brought from Judah? I have heard that the spirit of God is in you, that you possess brilliant knowledge and extraordinary wisdom."

—DANIEL 5:13–14

If we grow in our faith and our spiritual gifts, sooner or later we will be called into the presence of someone of influence. We should not be surprised when such opportunities arise, because God has worked this way throughout history. We are designed to manifest God's very character and thus draw people to God. Are we willing to become visible and vocal when others invite us to share with them what we know?

Daniel 5:1–6, 13–14, 16–17, 23–28
Daniel 3:62–67
Luke 21:12–19

• SAINT ANDREW DUNG-LAC, PRIEST AND MARTYR, AND HIS COMPANIONS,
MARTYRS • THANKSGIVING DAY •

*People will die of fright in anticipation of what is coming upon the
world, for the powers of the heavens will be shaken. . . . But when these
signs begin to happen, stand erect and raise your heads because your
redemption is at hand.*

—LUKE 21:26, 28

When the world is so shaken that people die of fright, we
are told to hold up our heads and wait to witness God's
work. If we were truly aware of what it means to be loved
by God, we would never be anxious or afraid.

Thanksgiving Day—proper Mass: In Thanksgiving to God (943–947), especially
Sirach 50:22–24
1 Corinthians 1:3–9
Luke 17:11–19

Daniel 6:12–28
Daniel 3:68–74
Luke 21:20–28

• SAINT CATHERINE OF ALEXANDRIA, VIRGIN AND MARTYR •

You dolphins and all water creatures, bless the Lord;
praise and exalt him above all forever.
All you birds of the air, bless the Lord;
praise and exalt him above all forever.
All you beasts, wild and tame, bless the Lord;
praise and exalt him above all forever.
—DANIEL 3:79–81

Try to observe animals more closely today. Imagine their sounds and movements as forms of praise to God. Whether playing, sleeping, or gathering food, they express, in some way, God's glory.

Daniel 7:2–14
Daniel 3:75–81
Luke 21:29–33

NOVEMBER 26

Then the kingship and dominion and majesty
of all the kingdoms under the heavens
shall be given to the holy people of the Most High,
Whose kingdom shall be everlasting:
all dominions shall serve and obey him.

—DANIEL 7:27

Each day of this life prepares us for a special destiny. As holy people of God, we will rule entire realms. This is good to remember when life's lessons are particularly hard. We learn now so that we can rule in eternity in wisdom and peace.

Daniel 7:15–27
Psalm 80
Luke 21:34–36

NOVEMBER 27

• FIRST SUNDAY OF ADVENT •

He will keep you firm to the end, irreproachable on the day of our Lord Jesus [Christ]. God is faithful, and by him you were called to fellowship with his Son, Jesus Christ our Lord.

—1 CORINTHIANS 1:8–9

Thank you, Lord, for taking responsibility for us. Even when we are weak and foolish, you keep us until the end. Even when we are not faithful, your faithfulness carries us to better days.

Isaiah 63:16–17, 19; 64:2–7
Psalm 80
1 Corinthians 1:3–9
Mark 13:33–37

For the peace of Jerusalem pray:
"May those who love you prosper! . . ."
For family and friends I say,
"May peace be yours."
For the house of the LORD, our God, I pray,
"May blessings be yours."
—PSALM 122:6, 8–9

Pray always. Pray for your country. Pray for your family and friends. Pray for your community of faith. Say words of blessing often. There is power in every blessing you utter.

Isaiah 2:1–5
Psalm 122
Matthew 8:5–11

———————————

NOVEMBER 29

He shows pity to the needy and the poor
and saves the lives of the poor.
From extortion and violence he frees them,
for precious is their blood in his sight.

—PSALM 72:13–14

Concern for the poor is described repeatedly in Scripture
as a chief trait of a righteous king. What if Christians
everywhere made a study of their leaders in light of this
one criterion: he or she looks out for the interests of the
poor and powerless?

Isaiah 11:1–10
Psalm 72
Luke 10:21–24

[T]he scripture says, "No one who believes in him will be put to shame." For there is no distinction between Jew and Greek; the same Lord is Lord of all, enriching all who call upon him.

—ROMANS 10:11–12

Some people have a hard time accepting Christians who are not part of their own group as fellow followers of Christ. In a story that illustrates this, a man dies and enters heaven, and an angel shows him around. Various courtyards are filled with groups of people from all over the world. But the man and the angel pass one room with a closed door. The angel opens it a bit so the man can see the people inside. "Why the closed door?" he asks. "Oh," replies the angel, "they think they are the only ones here."

Romans 10:9–18
Psalm 19
Matthew 4:18–22

DECEMBER 1

I was hard pressed and falling,
but the LORD came to my help.
The LORD, my strength and might,
came to me as savior.

—PSALM 118:13–14

God, you come to us as many things: father or mother,
judge, wise one, healer, even servant. But some days we are
almost overwhelmed by pressure, or we are teetering on
some dangerous edge. Thank you, on those days especially,
for being the One who reaches out and saves us.

Isaiah 26:1–6
Psalm 118
Matthew 7:21, 24–27

DECEMBER 2

I believe I shall enjoy the LORD's goodness
in the land of the living.
Wait for the LORD, take courage;
be stouthearted, wait for the LORD!
—PSALM 27:13–14

Mira had survived many trials during her eighty years, and nearly everyone at church adopted her as honorary Grandma. People came to her when they were discouraged. They wanted to know how Mira could keep going and have such joy. What was her secret? Her answer was simple: "If God is good enough to keep my future safe for me, then the least I can do is have a happy attitude while I wait."

Isaiah 29:17–24
Psalm 27
Matthew 9:27–31

DECEMBER 3

• SAINT FRANCIS XAVIER, PRIEST •

The LORD rebuilds Jerusalem,
gathers the dispersed of Israel, . . .
Numbers all the stars,
calls each of them by name.
—PSALM 147:2, 4

Tamara no longer trusted God to care about her. There seemed to be no relief from her never-ending divorce and custody battles. But one Sunday the psalm reading caught her attention, particularly the phrase about God calling each star by name. *He must know my name, too,* she thought, her eyes filling with tears. It was just a poetic phrase from an ancient book. But it lifted her spirits, and she was able to go on.

Isaiah 30:19–21, 23–26
Psalm 147
Matthew 9:35–10:1, 5–8

DECEMBER 4

[D]o not ignore this one fact, beloved, that with the Lord one day is like a thousand years and a thousand years like one day. The Lord does not delay his promise, as some regard "delay," but he is patient with you, not wishing that any should perish but that all should come to repentance.

—2 PETER 3:8–9

It's true that time seems to progress according to circumstances—flying by when we are carefree and barely moving when we're suffering. It's true, too, that time is a small matter to you, Lord, merely a characteristic that is tied to a physical universe. Help us live through every moment fully, understanding that past, present, and future are all one in the eternal scheme of things.

Isaiah 40:1–5, 9–11
Psalm 85
2 Peter 3:8–14
Mark 1:1–8

DECEMBER 5

A highway will be there,
called the holy way;
No one unclean may pass over it,
nor fools go astray on it. . . .
It is for those with a journey to make,
and on it the redeemed will walk.

—ISAIAH 35:8–9

Ahead of me stretches a road. I don't know what lies upon it, only that it is my road, the one that will take my soul on the journey it needs. And I know that my companions will be grace, hope, peace, courage, joy, love, adventure. My guide is Jesus, and the final destination is my home with God.

Isaiah 35:1–10
Psalm 85
Luke 5:17–26

DECEMBER 6

• SAINT NICHOLAS, BISHOP •

Like a shepherd he feeds his flock;
in his arms he gathers the lambs,
Carrying them in his bosom,
and leading the ewes with care.

—ISAIAH 40:11

Like St. Nicholas, the patron saint of children—who is popularly associated with Santa Claus—God cares for his children and provides for them. As we become children again during this holiday season, we can reflect on Isaiah's picture of God: a shepherd who cares for his flock with great detail and gentleness.

Isaiah 40:1–11
Psalm 96
Matthew 18:12–14

DECEMBER 7

• SAINT AMBROSE, BISHOP AND DOCTOR OF THE CHURCH •

Though young men faint and grow weary, . . .
[t]hey that hope in the LORD will renew their strength,
they will soar as with eagles' wings;

—ISAIAH 40:30–31

Isaiah's words could well describe the life of St. Ambrose, whose long career in service of the church involved peacemaking, protecting the poor, writing on doctrine and theology, and standing against emperors. Whatever our life callings and opportunities are, we, too, can gain strength from hope and thus live faithfully.

Isaiah 40:25–31
Psalm 103
Matthew 11:28–30

DECEMBER 8

Blessed be the God and Father of our Lord Jesus Christ, who has blessed us in Christ with every spiritual blessing in the heavens, as he chose us in him, before the foundation of the world, to be holy and without blemish before him.

—EPHESIANS 1:3–4

The immaculate conception puts Mary in a special category. Yet each of us has been chosen by God from the very beginning to be holy and "without blemish." As we celebrate the Blessed Virgin, we can also celebrate how glorious we have become in God's sight.

Genesis 3:9–15, 20
Psalm 98
Ephesians 1:3–6, 11–12
Luke 1:26–38

Friday

DECEMBER 9

• SAINT JUAN DIEGO, HERMIT •

I, the LORD, your God,
teach you what is for your good,
and lead you on the way you should go.
If you would hearken to my commandments,
your prosperity would be like a river,
and your vindication like the waves of the sea.

—ISAIAH 48:17–18

Every parent has said something like "If my kids would just
listen to me, they could avoid so much heartache!" God
has said this from earliest times. He said it to the Israelites
through the prophet Isaiah, and the same message comes
to us through our many teachers and prophets today. God
will teach us what is for our good.

Isaiah 48:17–19
Psalm 1
Matthew 11:16–19

"Elijah will indeed come and restore all things; but I tell you that Elijah has already come, and they did not recognize him but did to him whatever they pleased. . . ." Then the disciples understood that he was speaking to them of John the Baptist.

—MATTHEW 17:11–13

The Christian faith does not include belief in reincarnation; Christians believe that a person's soul remains distinct throughout eternity. John the Baptist did not come as Elijah, but rather they shared the same mission: to prepare God's people for special grace.

Sirach 48:1–4, 9–11
Psalm 80
Matthew 17:9–13

Do not quench the Spirit. Do not despise prophetic utterances. Test everything; retain what is good. Refrain from every kind of evil.

—1 THESSALONIANS 5:19–22

Holy Spirit, help us be people of spiritual depth and discernment. Don't let us be comfortable with religion that is superficial and with faith that is never tested and strengthened.

Isaiah 61:1–2, 10–11
Luke 1:46–50, 53–54
1 Thessalonians 5:16–24
John 1:6–8, 19–28

Sing and rejoice, O daughter Zion! See, I am coming to dwell among you, says the LORD. Many nations shall join themselves to the LORD on that day, and they shall be his people, and he will dwell among you, and you shall know that the LORD of hosts has sent me to you.

—ZECHARIAH 2:14–15

Lord, you have indeed come to dwell among many peoples so that they can claim you as their own. When Our Lady of Guadalupe appeared to a native Mexican, a population of indigenous people understood that you had chosen them for your own. You are not merely the God of conquering people, of a particular race, or of those who are rich and powerful.

Zechariah 2:14–17 or Revelation 11:19; 12:1–6, 10
Psalm 25
Luke 1:26–38 or 1:39–47 or any readings from the Common of the Blessed Virgin Mary, nos. 707–712

DECEMBER 13

• SAINT LUCY, VIRGIN AND MARTYR •

When John came to you in the way of righteousness, you did not believe him; but tax collectors and prostitutes did. Yet even when you saw that, you did not later change your minds and believe him.

—MATTHEW 21:32

Why do we avoid the truth? Why do we rationalize our way around what is simple and straightforward? Are we that proud? Do we have so much to lose by admitting that we need help and guidance? Usually the first people to turn to God are those who don't have much—those without resources or influence. What a shame that we can't respond to the holy until we are down-and-out.

Zephaniah 3:1–2, 9–13
Psalm 34
Matthew 21:28–32

DECEMBER 14

The disciples of John told him about all these things. John summoned two of his disciples and sent them to the Lord to ask, "Are you the one who is to come, or should we look for another?"

—LUKE 7:18–19

This was the same John the Baptist who first identified Jesus: "Behold, the Lamb of God, who takes away the sin of the world" (John 1:29). John was in prison when he sent his disciples to ask Jesus point-blank who he was. Maybe John was discouraged or depressed or just needed some confirmation of his faith. We can look to him or to St. John of the Cross, another tortured saint, when our souls are in pain or confusion.

Isaiah 45:6–8, 18, 21–25
Psalm 85
Luke 7:18–23

Thursday

DECEMBER 15

Complacent, I once said,
"I shall never be shaken."
LORD, when you showed me favor
I stood like the mighty mountains.
But when you hid your face
I was struck with terror.

—PSALM 30:7–8

When life is going well, I forget how much I need you. I assume that my good fortune is a result of my own will and work. I grow too confident of myself and too forgetful of you. All it takes is one bad day to send me reeling back into prayer. A small bit of suffering reminds me that everything good in my life is a gift from you.

Isaiah 54:1–10
Psalm 30
Luke 7:24–30

DECEMBER 16

[John] was a burning and shining lamp, and for a while you were content to rejoice in his light. But I have testimony greater than John's.
—JOHN 5:35–36

God gives us "shining lamps," people in whom God's love burns. We meet such a person and talk for a few moments and walk away feeling refreshed or challenged or healed. Thank you, Lord, for all the living testimonies of your love who walk through our lives.

Isaiah 56:1–3, 6–8
Psalm 67
John 5:33–36

DECEMBER 17

Thus the total number of generations from Abraham to David is fourteen generations; from David to the Babylonian exile, fourteen generations; from the Babylonian exile to the Messiah, fourteen generations.

—MATTHEW 1:17

To please her great-aunt, Sarah researched their distant relatives in Belgium. But her interest was piqued as she uncovered information about early generations of her family. She began to see herself as not merely a twenty-something in California but one name in a strand of many that stretched across at least four other countries and two hundred years. Her life was part of a larger destiny, and her days and years seemed more important now.

Genesis 49:2, 8–10
Psalm 72
Matthew 1:1–17

DECEMBER 18

• FOURTH SUNDAY OF ADVENT •

Thus says the LORD: Should you build me a house to dwell in?
—2 SAMUEL 7:5

God's question to King David is a good reminder: God does not "dwell" in buildings or need shelter from the weather. People sometimes feel the need to put God in a specific place, but God dwells with us wherever we are.

2 Samuel 7:1–5, 8–12, 14, 16
Psalm 89
Romans 16:25–27
Luke 1:26–38

DECEMBER 19

The woman bore a son and named him Samson. The boy grew up and
the LORD blessed him; the spirit of the LORD first stirred him in
Mahaneh-dan, which is between Zorah and Eshtaol.

—JUDGES 13:24–25

Where did the Spirit first "stir" you? Do you remember a
date and place? Did a phrase strike you to the core, or did
you sense a great kindness or wisdom that was too
powerful to ignore? Spend some time today remembering
the Holy Spirit's stirring in your life.

Judges 13:2–7, 24–25
Psalm 71
Luke 1:5–25

⇒ 389 ⇐

DECEMBER 20

Who may go up the mountain of the LORD?
Who can stand in his holy place?
The clean of hand and pure of heart,
who are not devoted to idols,
who have not sworn falsely.

—PSALM 24:3–4

God, how can I get to where you are? What does it take?
What do you require of me, a frail human being? Is there a
secret code I need to crack, a new vocabulary I must learn?
No? You want my heart and mind? That seems too
simple—and it is. You're asking for my whole self, and it
will take me a lifetime to understand how to give that self
to you.

Isaiah 7:10–14
Psalm 24
Luke 1:26–38

• SAINT PETER CANISIUS, PRIEST AND DOCTOR OF THE CHURCH •

From heaven the LORD looks down
and observes the whole human race. . . .
The one who fashioned the hearts of them all
knows all their works.

—PSALM 33:13, 15

When the factory's most complicated mechanism broke down, the machine's manufacturer sent a bent old man to repair it. The factory president immediately called the manufacturer, demanding that they send their most capable serviceman. "Sir, you have the most capable," was the reply. "That old man *built* your machine."

Song of Songs 2:8–14 or Zephaniah 3:14–18
Psalm 33
Luke 1:39–45

Thursday

DECEMBER 22

The LORD puts to death and gives life;
he casts down to the nether world;
he raises up again.
The LORD makes poor and makes rich,
he humbles, he also exalts.

—1 SAMUEL 2:6–7

My culture teaches me to take charge of my own life, to
be "proactive" and assertive, to make plans and work
toward my goals. But holy people through the ages have
understood that ultimately our lives are not our own.
Will we acknowledge this and be humble enough to
honor God of the universe? Can we make room in our
philosophies for worship?

1 Samuel 1:24–28
1 Samuel 2:1, 4–8
Luke 1:46–56

• SAINT JOHN OF KANTY, PRIEST •

[W]ho will endure the day of his coming?
And who can stand when he appears?
For he is like the refiner's fire.

—MALACHI 3:2

When Karen gave her life to God, she had no idea that her conversion would take her far beyond healing and forgiveness. She has been a Christian for sixty years now, and she often says, "The good Lord will work with you until the imperfections are gone and you are exactly the glorious creature he intended. The refining process isn't always easy or pleasant, but how can we expect to spend eternity in God's holy presence if we aren't holy ourselves?"

Malachi 3:1–4, 23–24
Psalm 25
Luke 1:57–66

Happy the people who know you, LORD,
who walk in the radiance of your face.

—PSALM 89:16

Because Jesus was born as one of us, we were able to know God in a new, vivid way. God indeed had a face that people could see—a human face and personality that brought us into intimate contact with our Creator and Father. Thank you, Lord, for revealing your very self to us.

2 Samuel 7:1–5, 8–12, 14, 16
Psalm 89
Luke 1:67–79

Sunday

DECEMBER 25

THE NATIVITY OF THE LORD • CHRISTMAS •

[T]he grace of God has appeared, saving all and training us to reject godless ways and worldly desires and to live temperately, justly, and devoutly in this age, as we await the blessed hope, the appearance of the glory of the great God and of our savior Jesus Christ, who gave himself for us to deliver us from all lawlessness and to cleanse for himself a people as his own, eager to do what is good.

—TITUS 2:11–14

Jesus has saved us from our sins. He has taught us how to live. He has given us every resource for abundant life. And he has gathered us into the divine family of God. These are the joys we celebrate on Christmas Day.

395 ⇐

Vigil:
Isaiah 62:1–5
Psalm 89
Acts 13:16–17, 22–25
Matthew 1:1–25 or 1:18–25

Midnight:
Isaiah 9:1–6
Psalm 96
Titus 2:11–14
Luke 2:1–14

Dawn:
Isaiah 62:11–12
Psalm 97
Titus 3:4–7
Luke 2:15–20

Day:
Isaiah 52:7–10
Psalm 98
Hebrews 1:1–6
John 1:1–18 or 1:1–5, 9–14

*Brother will hand over brother to death, and the father his child;
children will rise up against parents and have them put to death. You
will be hated by all because of my name, but whoever endures to the end
will be saved.*

—MATTHEW 10:21–22

These are hard words. Am I willing to stay with God even
if that means abandoning those closest to me? I hope it
never comes to that, but I know that sometimes our loved
ones do not understand our spiritual path. My spiritual
path is the way I must go. No one can walk it for me, and
only by walking it myself will I find my way to my destiny
in God.

Acts 6:8–10; 7:54–59
Psalm 31
Matthew 10:17–22

Tuesday

DECEMBER 27

• SAINT JOHN, APOSTLE AND EVANGELIST •

[T]he life was made visible;
we have seen it and testify to it
and proclaim to you the eternal life
that was with the Father and was made visible to us.

—1 JOHN 1:2

John was one of the three apostles in Jesus' "inner circle."
In John's later years he was exiled to the Isle of Patmos; the
visions he had there were written down and have survived
as the book of Revelation. John simply reported what was
made visible to him. This is all that God asks of any of us:
to testify to what we have seen and experienced.

1 John 1:1–4
Psalm 97
John 20:1–8

⋺ 398 ⋷

DECEMBER 28

[I]f anyone does sin, we have an Advocate with the Father, Jesus Christ the righteous one. He is expiation for our sins, and not for our sins only but for those of the whole world.

—1 JOHN 2:1–2

God, I don't understand how you can wipe out sins that are so heinous, such as Herod's massacre of the children in Bethlehem in his attempt to kill Jesus. How do you heal the genocide of millions? How do you make right the torture of those who love you? I don't expect to understand; please help me trust your goodness.

1 John 1:5–2:2
Psalm 124
Matthew 2:13–18

DECEMBER 29

Tremble before God, all the earth;
say among the nations: The LORD is king.
—PSALM 96:9–10

St. Thomas Becket was killed because he opposed rulers and held fast to his teachings and duties as a spiritual leader. Sometimes God's people have to remind earthly rulers that the Lord is king. Pray today for people of faith around the world who are positioned to speak for God, especially those who speak before powerful people.

1 John 2:3–11
Psalm 96
Luke 2:22–35

My son, take care of your father when he is old;
grieve him not as long as he lives.
Even if his mind fail, be considerate with him;
revile him not in the fullness of your strength.

—SIRACH 3:12–13

Chris and his father had battled some over the years, but when his father needed to live with someone after his stroke, Chris moved his dad to his home. During those months, Chris got to know his dad as a person with a history of his own that included many trials and achievements that Chris had known little about. When his dad was well enough to leave, Chris felt that he had said good-bye to not only a father but also a friend.

Sirach 3:2–7, 12–14 or Genesis 15:1–6; 21:1–3
Psalm 128 or 105
Colossians 3:12–21 or 3:12–17 or Hebrews 11:8, 11–12, 17–19
Luke 2:22–40 or 2:22, 39–40

In the beginning was the Word,
and the Word was with God,
and the Word was God.
He was in the beginning with God.
All things came to be through him,
and without him nothing came to be.

—JOHN 1:1–3

Lord Jesus, we cannot experience creation without experiencing you. We cannot know God without knowing you. And when we trace our origins, you are at the beginning of our being. May we recognize you in every beauty, in every thought, in every spark of faith.

1 John 2:18–21
Psalm 96
John 1:1–18